English ⌗ Heritage
Book of
Fountains Abbey

English ⌗ Heritage
Book of
Fountains Abbey

Glyn Coppack

B. T. Batsford Ltd/English Heritage
London

This book is dedicated to the memory of the late Roy Gilyard-Beer whose life-long study of Fountains Abbey has provided the basis for my own work on the site. Without his encouragement and criticism I would never have had the courage to take up where he left off and tell the story of such a remarkable monument to monasticism and the people who were responsible for it.

And to Denny, Hannah and Tomas who have lived with Fountains Abbey for longer than they care to remember.

Typeset by
Goodfellow & Egan Phototypesetting Ltd, Cambridge
and printed in Great Britain by
The Bath Press, Bath

Published by B. T. Batsford Ltd
4 Fitzhardinge Street, London W1H 0AH

A CIP catalogue record for this book is available from the British Library

ISBN 0 7134 6858 0 (cased)
0 7134 6859 9 (limp)

Contents

Illustrations

Colour plates

Preface

There are standing remains of some 200 medieval monasteries in England, less than a quarter of the total built. The finest of these is undoubtedly Fountains Abbey, a roofless ruin since 1540, set in an important eighteenth-century managed landscape. The abbey and the park of Studley Royal in which it now stands are owned by the National Trust and were designated a World Heritage Site by UNESCO in 1988. Together they receive in excess of 300,000 visitors a year, a certain sign of the significance the general public affords them, but the very opposite of what was intended.

When a small band of monks came to Skelldale in the mid-winter of 1132 they had little notion of what they were starting. Theirs was a frontier settlement, a mission centre for the young Cistercian Order, set 'far from the concourse of men' where monks could follow the rule of St Benedict in communion with nature far from the distractions of the world outside. They settled in the wood of Herleshowe, for as St Bernard taught 'you will find in woods something you will never find in books – stones and trees will teach you a lesson you never heard from masters in the schools'. It was to be a hard lesson but a profitable one. The rags-to-riches story of Fountains Abbey paralleled the meteoric success of the Cistercian Order itself, and Fountains provides one of the finest examples of the rise and decline of the order in Europe, where success sapped the spirituality that drove it. Within 50 years of its foundation, powered by religious fervour and funded by the income of a substantial and well-managed estate, Fountains was the principal house of the order in England and rivalled the first daughter-houses of Cîteaux itself.

The story of Fountains Abbey is written not only in contemporary documents but also in the surviving fabric of its buildings and in its buried archaeology. This story has been gradually unravelled over the past 20 years as English Heritage and before that the Department of the Environment conserved the ruins and recorded the fabric of the monument. This book presents for the first time the results of that work which have led to a total reappraisal of the monastery's development, and made Fountains the most completely understood Cistercian monastery. Our knowledge remains imperfect and the full story can never be known for the site is an incomplete shell that is only well documented for parts of its history. The work of conservation and study continues and will not be completed for another 20 years and it is likely that much more information than is currently available will come to light. In particular, the greater part of the earliest monastic buildings remain unexcavated, a wonderful resource for future generations whose techniques of excavation and information retrieval will be much more sophisticated than our own. All the same, Fountains remains the most intensively studied Cistercian house in any part of Europe.

The site has been the subject of antiquarian study since the seventeenth century and of archaeological research since the late eighteenth. Its study by Richard Walbran, Gordon Hill, Arthur Reeve and Sir William St John Hope in the nineteenth century placed Fountains in the forefront of monastic studies where it remains today. In the present century, that study was continued by John Bilson, the Revd A.W. Oxford, W.T. Lancaster, Roy Gilyard-Beer, B. Waites, R.A. Donkin and David

Michelmore. By the late 1970s it could reasonably be assumed that there was little more to learn about the site, its history, and its economy. At the time I would have believed this myself, but as events have since proved, my judgement was poor indeed.

I owe my own involvement with Fountains Abbey to John Weaver who invited me to undertake excavations in advance of the Department of the Environment conservation programme from 1977, the first major campaign of excavation since the late 1880s. The success of that work was greatly enhanced by the generosity of the late Roy Gilyard-Beer who shared his unrivalled understanding of the monument with me. It was particularly excavation within the church in 1979–80 which revolutionized the interpretation of the surviving fabric and pointed the way for future research.

From 1983 to 1989, I was additionally fortunate to be the Inspector of Ancient Monuments responsible for Fountains, during which time a detailed survey of the fabric was begun, first undertaken by Judith Roebuck and latterly by Keith Emerick. Both have willingly shared their knowledge of the site with me and provided a sounding-board against which I have tried out many of my own ideas. They have both allowed me to use their work in advance of their own publication, for which I am particularly grateful. Without their work, this book would not have been possible. Of course, English Heritage has no copyright on research at Fountains and the monument continues to be the focus of international study. I have drawn widely on the work of others as they have drawn on my work. In particular, two scholars deserve my particular thanks: Stuart Harrison who has made an extensive study of the loose architectural detail from the site and made available his unpublished drawings, and Professor Peter Fergusson who has taught me to see Fountains in the wider significance of the Cistercian Order. Both have helped me to understand the monument in ways that do not come easily to an archaeologist and have also corrected my worst errors of fact and interpretation. They bear no responsibility for those that remain. Others have helped in different ways: Dr Christopher Young ensured that the programme of archaeological research that lies behind this book was funded adequately and allowed to continue; my successor Jim Lang who has continued the work I began; and the National Trust and English Heritage teams caring for Fountains, who appreciate the importance of a proper study of the monument as it is conserved for posterity. My debt to scholarship is no less great. I have benefited from the advice and encouragement of many scholars, among them the late Professor Maurice Barley, Dr Peter Addyman, Dr Philip Dixon, Dr Christopher Norton, Dr Jennie Stopford, Dr Stuart Wrathmell, Steve Moorhouse, Dr Susan Wright, Susan Hirst, Professor David Walsh, Dr Terryl Kinder and Richard Halsey. I have freely quarried from the work of others, and this is acknowledged in the text, though the interpretation is mine alone.

In the production of this book I have had the invaluable assistance of Karen Guffog, Kate Morton and Judith Dobie of English Heritage who have prepared many of the line drawings, and of Simon Hayfield whose line drawings were prepared for publication in the early 1980s and which are reused here. Many of the photographs derive from the English Heritage Photographic Library or from my own collection. Others are acknowledged in the captions.

Fountains Abbey remains for me the most remarkable of monastic sites, a testimony to those who built it and to those responsible for its care today. This book marks my own contribution to the study of a monument which will continue to excite and give pleasure to many future generations. Now its potential is realized, I hope it will continue to be exploited by scholars and visitors alike.

Glyn Coppack
Goxhill
27 December 1991

1

The new soldiers of Christ

On 27 December 1132, Archbishop Thurstan of York brought a group of 13 monks from York to the valley of the river Skell 6 km (4 miles) to the west of Ripon. Here he gave them the site to build a monastery, a wild and inhospitable place, more fitting to be the lair of wild beasts than of men. Initially, the monks sheltered under the rocks of the valley, and then under an elm tree. From this unpromising beginning grew the great Cistercian abbey of Fountains (**colour plate 1**). How this came about, and how Fountains came to be one of the greatest abbeys of its order and indeed one of the most important monastic sites in Europe, is truly remarkable. Contemporary documents, surviving buildings and the evidence of archaeology together make Fountains Abbey the most informative of any Cistercian abbey in Europe, and show clearly the development of the most remarkable monastic reform movement in Christendom.

The ruins of Fountains Abbey comprise one of the finest and most extensive monastic sites in Europe and reflect the wealth and ambitions of the Cistercian monks who lived there for just over four centuries. What can be seen today is no more than the skeleton of an abbey; all the furnishings and fittings, most of the wall-painting, and the silence of monastic life have gone, to be replaced by eighteenth-century landscaping and twentieth-century visitors. Enough remains, however, to enable the recreation of much that has been lost by spoliation and weathering, and to reconstruct the story of Fountains' development. Although it was to become the greatest of Britain's Cistercian abbeys, its present appearance belies its early history, for the first years of the monastery's existence were fraught with poverty and

uncertainty. The ruins that survive are in fact the remains of the third abbey to be built on the site; each represents a stage in the development of the Cistercian order internationally.

The origins of the Cistercian Order

It is not in Skelldale that the story begins, for the origins of Fountains Abbey can be traced back to a strangely similar occurrence in France. The tenth and eleventh centuries were a time of reform in the monastic world, as Benedictine monks attempted to improve their ideals and their liturgies. In 910, the foundation of a new abbey at Cluny near Mâcon in Burgundy had marked a revival of monastic life. Originally a house of Benedictine monks, Cluny benefited from a series of very able abbots who insisted on a stricter observance of the early sixth-century Benedictine rule, making Cluny the centre of an influential monastic revival not only in France but throughout Europe. What began at Cluny was to continue as other groups of monks sought a more exacting way to reach God through prayer and manual work. In 1098, a group of dissenting monks left the Cluniac abbey of Molesme in southern Burgundy, frustrated in an attempt to bring their lives into an even stricter accordance with the precepts of St Benedict that were central to monastic life in medieval Europe. Led by their prior Robert, 21 monks left Molesme to build a new monastery where they could enjoy a harsh but simple life. They called their new house, built on swampy land 22.5 km (14 miles) south of Dijon, the Newminster (*monasterium novum*). In Latin, the common monastic language, the site was called *Cistertium* from *cisterna*, a marsh. In modern French it is called Cîteaux.

Atrium

Lay cemetery

1 *The tenth-century buildings of the second monastery at Cluny, reconstructed by Kenneth Conant, show the layout and scale of monastic buildings against which the first Cistercians reacted.*

Benedictine monasticism was almost 700 years old when Cîteaux was founded and had grown away from the way of life its founder had intended. By the early years of the ninth century, the medieval concept of the monastery was fully developed, with a great church and cloister ranges providing the enclosure for the religious at the centre of a supporting array of courts and service buildings. Monasteries were wealthy institutions supported by vast agricultural estates and their wealth went into the creation of fine buildings and developing liturgies. The St Gall plan, the schematic design for a new Benedictine monastery in Switzerland, drawn up in about 820, shows the scale and complexity that had become the norm for an important monastery. At the centre was the cloister, with its garden, the very heart of monastic life, with the common dormitory on its east side, the refectory on its south side and a store house on the west. The fourth side of the cloister was closed by a great church, the largest of all the buildings of the monastery. Surrounding these core buildings was a whole series of smaller but no less important buildings: kitchens, brewhouses, bakehouses, smithy, cooper's shop, animal houses, infirmary, gardens and cemetery. Not only monks lived in the monastery, but also their servants and workmen, and the whole was divided into three strictly controlled parts: the 'house', restricted to the religious; the Inner Court which was a semi-public area providing for guests; and the Outer Court which was the service area of the monastery where animals were kept, grain stored and industry practised. Whilst the cloister buildings were quiet and provided seclusion, the Inner and Outer Courts were rather noisier and distracting and the latter area was occasionally unpleasant. The aim was to make the monastery efficient, self-supporting and self-perpetuating, supported by a network of agricultural estates.

Efficiency brought wealth, and the only outlet for surplus money was building. At Cluny this had resulted in the construction of a monumental church (1), the centre of a highly developed ritual. The dissenting monks from Molesme wanted none of this, but sought to return to first principles, redefining monasticism and building crude timber buildings with their own hands. In 1099, Robert and half his followers were forced to return to Molesme, but in spite of this serious set-back the new community of *Cistertium* survived and began the building of a simple stone church and cloister which were sufficiently complete to be consecrated in 1106. Stone buildings imply both the support of patrons and permanence of the community, though there is no suggestion that at this point the monks saw themselves as anything other than Benedictines living in stricter accordance with St Benedict's Rule than their Cluniac brothers of Molesme.

It was an Englishman, Stephen Harding (**colour plate 2**), who forced the pace of reform in the new abbey. Initially a monk of Sherborne in Dorset, he had abandoned his cloister and travelled widely. In 1085 he had returned to monastic life at Molesme following a pilgrimage to Rome, and rose to become the sub-prior of the house. According to a fellow west-countryman William of Malmesbury, writing his *Gesta Regum Anglorum* in 1122–3, it was Harding who had initially been responsible for the dissent at Molesme. In 1109 he was elected abbot of *Cistertium*, a post he was to hold until his death in 1135. His strict interpretation of the Benedictine rule and particularly its insistence on poverty and manual labour almost destroyed the community, for disease and death seriously reduced numbers.

The new monastery's reputation for discipline and simple living was its salvation, however, attracting many recruits of exceptional ability, to the extent that a second monastery had to be established at La Ferté in 1113. A further colony was established at Pontigny in 1114, and two more at Morimond and Clairvaux in 1115. With Cîteaux, these four colonies were to form the core of the most successful monastic reform movement of the Middle Ages (2). By 1119 there were five more monasteries established and the time had come formally to create a new Order; this was to be known from *Cistertium* as the Cistercian Order.

The creation of a rule

The rapid growth of Cîteaux and its four daughter-houses required the development of a monastic philosophy, and it was again Stephen Harding who was responsible for the early codification of the communities' ideals, spiritual, social and architectural. His approach was fundamental, taking the rule that St Benedict had written for his monastery at Monte Casino in the early years of the sixth century, but also going back to the earlier teachings of St Basil and John Cassian. Central to life at Cîteaux and her colonies were two documents: the Little Introduction (*Exordium Parvum*), an account of the foundation of Cîteaux, and the Charter of Love (*Carta Caritatis*), an outline of the Cistercians' constitution, both largely the work of Harding and dating to around 1119 although they contain material from earlier legislative documents. They set an uncompromising insistence on poverty, simplicity of life and the need to separate the communities physically from the outside world. The dependence on the outside world for financial support, that is the income from manors and churches given by patrons to support religious communities, was seen as the cause of worldliness in other orders that distracted monks from their prime objective, to serve God by prayer and manual work.

To prevent disturbance, the Cistercians placed their monasteries away from other settlements, 'far from the concourse of men', and sought to be self-sufficient, renouncing all cash revenues and feudal ties. Their economy, without which they could not survive, was to be land-based. To achieve such an economy without being reliant on feudal labour, the Cistercians developed the concept of lay brothers or *conversi* who would work their estates whilst bound by monastic discipline. Older orders had used small numbers of lay brothers but it was the Cistercians who developed the idea that they should be recruited in large numbers to service their abbeys. They were effectively second-class monks, and offered on a large scale a chance previously denied to the uneducated labouring and servant classes to enter monastic life. The rapid growth of the order and its capacity to support itself was very much due to this concept. While the presence of lay brothers enabled the order to develop a highly centralized method of farming (see Chapter 5), the need to accommodate two separate communities within a single monastery required a

2 *The location of Cîteaux, her first daughter-houses and other major houses mentioned in the text.*

fundamental re-arrangement of the traditional monastic plan.

St Benedict had required his monks to divide their lives into three parts: the saying of the church offices (*opus Dei*); spiritual reading and meditation (*lectio divina*); and manual labour (*opus manuum*). By the end of the eleventh century this three-way division had virtually disappeared. Ulrich, writing of life at Cluny itself around 1090, tells that so much time was taken up by the church offices which had become such highly developed rituals that the monks had no time for manual labour and hardly any time for reading. The Cistercians ruthlessly redefined the monastic timetable.

Beginning with the *opus Dei* they cut all additions, with the sole exception of the morning Mass, to the outline provided by St Benedict. Ceremonial was reduced, and musical chant simplified. With time spent in church reduced, both reading and manual work could be restored. Importantly, an opportunity was also provided for private prayer.

To ensure the stability of these reforms, the *Carta Caritatis* provided the model for a central authority within the order that remains a masterpiece of planning. Each year, every abbot was to attend a general chapter at Cîteaux to enforce collective discipline and to enact statutes by which the development and direction of the order was to be controlled. Additionally, a cellular structure was created by which abbeys were arranged in 'families' headed by Cîteaux and its four original colonies. Each new monastery was the responsibility of the house it was founded from, and the abbot of that house was required to visit the colony or 'daughter-house' annually. Papal consent was obtained to exempt Cistercian monasteries from visitation and correction by diocesan bishops, ensuring that no outside influence could distract the movement of reform. So successful was this reform that within forty years of the foundation of Cîteaux's first daughter-house of La Ferté there were 339 monasteries within the order, a number which had risen to 525 by the close of the twelfth century. It is difficult now to appreciate the missionary zeal of Stephen Harding's 'new soldiers of Christ', the name they were given very early in their history.

Their strict discipline and asceticism appealed strongly to the aristocracy who formed the European military class, though they did not necessarily impress other monks. Abbot Peter the Venerable of Cluny was appalled by the Cistercians, writing in about 1127 that 'it is unbecoming that monks which are the fine linen of the sanctuary should be begrimed with dirt and bent down with rustic labours'. To the Benedictine William of Malmesbury, however, 'the Cistercians . . . are a model for all, a mirror for the diligent, a spur to the indolent'. Rejecting the black habits of the Benedictines and Cluniacs, the Cistercians wore undyed or white habits (**colour plate 3**), and became commonly known as 'White Monks'. Their lay brothers had brown habits to distinguish them (**colour plate 4**). Both were forbidden undershirts and

breeches, an unheard of austerity in the colder climate of northern Europe. Their diet was sparse and unremittingly vegetarian, their life was undoubtedly harsh, and to a certain extent anti-intellectual. However, it provided in the words of St Aelred of Rievaulx 'everywhere peace, everywhere serenity, and a marvellous freedom from the tumult of the world'.

St Bernard of Clairvaux

The Cistercian way of life attracted men of outstanding ability to the cloister, none more remarkable than a young Burgundian nobleman Bernard des Fontaines who entered Cîteaux with a group of his followers in 1113. Bernard's progression from novice to abbot of the daughter-house of Clairvaux in less than three years was nothing short of remarkable and as Bernard of Clairvaux he was eventually to replace St Stephen Harding as the driving force of the order (**colour plate 5**). The fraudulent alteration of Cistercian documents after St Bernard's death in 1153 has tended to take the credit for much of the reform from Stephen Harding, but the two men were very different in their reforming zeal. Harding was a monks' monk, while Bernard of Clairvaux took the influence of the Cistercian reform to a wider audience. He combined the two qualities of great austerity and unbounded energy, and was 'the counsellor of Popes and Kings'. It is difficult today to decide how much Bernard contributed to the development of the order, but his sermons, letters and his biography, the *Vita Prima*, edited by Geoffroi d'Auxerre tell us something of his character and achievements. All have to be studied with caution, and particularly the biography which, though begun during Bernard's lifetime was conceived as hagiography and not objective history. Some of it was clearly written with the benefit of hindsight!

For our purposes, the most important document is Bernard's *Apologia ad Guilielmum* (Discourse to William), which was written to the Benedictine William of St Thiery in the mid-1120s to justify the Cistercians' attack on the sumptuous buildings and excessive rituals of Cluny and which gives an insight into contemporary Cistercian ideology (**3**). He wrote of 'the immense height of the churches, their immoderate length, their superfluous breadth, costly polishing and strange designs that, while they attract the eye of the worshipper, hinder

3 *The great third church at Cluny, begun at the close of the eleventh century, appalled St Bernard by its ostentation and distracting ornament. Only the south transept has survived, but when complete it was the greatest monastic church in Europe.*

his attention', which would suggest that the Cistercians themselves favoured the opposite. He fulminated equally about great brass candlesticks, immoderate dress and rich food. Here he seems to have gone beyond Stephen Harding's philosophy and set a standard to which his order should direct itself. Some scholars have seen in St Bernard's criticism the seeds of Cistercian architectural development which is today particularly discernible within the family of Clairvaux, for the order was to build simple and unadorned churches that reflected Bernard's puritanism.

At the time that the *Apologia* was written, however, the Cistercians had yet to begin the building of major churches, and Bernard's com-ments reflect the deliberately small and austere churches that the order had at first adopted. It was not until a great new church was built at Clairvaux between 1135 and 1145 that a model existed of the 'Bernardine' church which has come to be accepted as the culmination of Bernard's architectural philosophy and which is clearly the model for the earliest surviving churches of the Clairvaux family in England. The building of this great new church was only agreed to by Bernard after much soul-searching but it was needed to house his rapidly growing community, and he always remembered the first buildings at Clairvaux with deep affection.

Bernard was a great organizer who saw the Cistercian reform as a missionary cause to be carefully planned and executed, building up the family of Clairvaux with a military precision in which he took a direct interest. Under his direction, Clairvaux began to outshine Cîteaux itself, and by his death in 1153 some 159 monasteries out of a total of 339 daughter-houses belonged to its filiation.

The mission to England

In 1131, Abbot Bernard of Clairvaux began the systematic colonization of northern England and Scotland. Writing to Henry I of England, Bernard claimed 'In your land there is an outpost of my Lord and your Lord, an outpost he has preferred to die for than to lose. I have proposed to occupy it and I am sending men from my army who will, if it is not displeasing to you, claim it, recover it, and restore it with a strong hand.' Emissaries sent with the letter were to survey the new site and report back to Clairvaux on its suitability. Behind the letter were the actions of Walter Espec, Lord of Helmsley and a Royal Justiciar, a vassal of both Henry I of England and King David of Scotland. Espec was no stranger to monastic reform. Following Henry's example he had brought a colony of Augustinians to Kirkham in Yorkshire in 1121–2, and he was now interested in settling the militant Cistercians on his lands with the support of his two feudal lords and the reformist Archbishop of York, Thurstan. A small colony of Yorkshire monks had entered Clairvaux and perhaps we should also see their desire to return to their homeland with the seeds of the Cistercian reform.

The Cistercians had already settled at Waverley in Surrey in 1128 with the support of William Giffard, Bishop of Winchester, the colony coming from l'Aumone in Normandy, of the family of Cîteaux. Bernard appears willingly to have grasped the chance to establish the family of Clairvaux in the north, almost in competition to Waverley which was to colonize southern Britain and Ireland. Both houses were to take advantage of wild, inhospitable and uncultivated land, areas ideal for Cistercian expansion.

On 5 March 1132, a colony of 12 Clairvaux monks led by their abbot, William, a scholar from York who had entered Clairvaux and served as Bernard's secretary, was settled in the valley of the river Rye 3.2km (2 miles) from Espec's castle of Helmsley. The foundation of Rievaulx Abbey as it was soon to be called caused an immediate explosion of monastic fervour in the north of England. Particularly affected were the two great Benedictine establishments, the cathedral priory of Durham and York Abbey, both rich houses with a growing reputation for worldliness. Both were ripe for the Cistercian reform, but it was at York that the missionary Cistercians had their greatest

effect. Their reputation of sanctity, poverty and simplicity appealed to six members of the York community, Ranulf, Thomas, Gamel, Hamo, Walter and Gregory, who, led by the sacrist Richard, began to press their ageing abbot Geoffrey for the return of their house to sound Benedictine values.

Dissent at York Abbey

Abbot Geoffrey was not prepared to see his authority questioned or his abbey reformed. Although the dispute first came to light in April, it dragged on throughout the summer of 1132 and the original group of dissenters was joined by the prior, another Richard, the sub-prior Gervase, Geoffrey, Robert of Subella, Radulf, Alexander and Robert, a former monk of Whitby. It was not until 28 June 1132 that Prior Richard put the case of the would-be reformers to the abbot in writing. The abbot delayed his reply until after 8 September, but the dispute had reached the ears of Archbishop Thurstan who resolved, as was his right, to visit the abbey and resolve the situation on 6 October. By then 13 members of the community were calling for reform and there seemed little hope of compromise. Abbot Geoffrey gathered support from the heads of other Benedictine and Cluniac houses and when the Archbishop arrived there was a brawl in the cloister as these black monks tried to prevent his officials entering the chapter-house. Thurstan had little choice but to place the abbey under an interdict and to take the dissenting monks into his own protection in his palace at York. There they remained until Christmas when they accompanied Thurstan to Ripon. Two days later, they were taken to Skelldale and Fountains Abbey was established. In addition to a plot of land for the abbey itself, Thurstan provided an endowment of two carucates of land at nearby Sutton to support the community. Prior Richard was elected the first abbot of the new monastery on the same day.

The earliest years of Fountains Abbey

The earliest history of Fountains is known from an eye-witness account recorded by brother Hugh of Kirkstall around 1206. Abbot John of York, mindful of the Cistercian tradition of recording the 'official' history of each monastery, advised Hugh to consult Serlo, then a monk of Kirkstall who was in his ninety-ninth year and who had been a member of the early

Fountains community. Although he had not entered Fountains until 1137, he had been in York at the time of the dispute and was related to some of the dissidents. He remained at Fountains until March 1147 when he left as one of the group who were eventually to settle a daughter-house at Kirkstall, and up to that date he would have shared the experiences of the founding community in their formative years. Thereafter, his story was based on information received. It is less detailed, and is admitted to include the memories of others. Hugh and Serlo's history, the *Narratio de fundatione Fontanis monasterii* (The Story of the Foundation of Fountain Abbey) is a remarkably informative document, despite the fact that it shows Serlo to have been a true Cistercian, indifferent to buildings and the passing of time. The few dates given are interpolated by Hugh from other sources, for Serlo was content with 'after some days' or 'not long afterwards'. His phrases are also typical of his Cistercian indoctrination, for they are taken directly from the Vulgate and early Cistercian manuscripts. How much of the similarity between Serlo's story and the early histories of Molesme, Cîteaux and Clairvaux results from coincidence, deliberate emulation or an unconscious wish to strengthen the story, we will never know, but the parallels that emerge are truly remarkable.

The Benedictines who settled Fountains were not provided with any shelter by the Archbishop; instead they were forced to shift as best they could in difficult circumstances. Sheltering first among the rocks and caves of the valley, they later sought the shelter of a great elm tree where they built a hut of wattles and turf. Although Thurstan had protected the monks for three months he had not provided the temporary buildings required for the settlement of any Cistercian abbey and which he must have seen when he attended the foundation ceremony at Rievaulx. Their planting in Skelldale must have been the result of careful thought, for the site proved to be ideal, and the lack of temporary buildings should be seen in the context that the monks were not yet Cistercian and therefore not subject to that Order's discipline. Indeed, they modelled their settlement on that of another Benedictine in Yorkshire. Benedict of Auxerre settled below an oak tree called *Stribac* on the bank of the river Ouse in 1068 to found the abbey of Selby, and it

may have been the choice of the Fountains monks to seek the hardest possible beginning for their house.

The hut of wattles and turf was shortly followed by the creation of a garden for manual labour and an oratory for prayer, and it was from this rudimentary monastery that emissaries were sent to Clairvaux to seek admission into the order early in 1133. Its site in the valley is uncertain, though John Leland recorded a tradition current in 1540 that the elm tree still survived, and was thus unlikely to be on the site of the later monastery buildings, and as recently as the late eighteenth century, a rotted stump called the 'Fountains Elm' was recorded 457m (1500ft) east of the present abbey buildings by Christopher Husband, grandfather of the historian Richard Walbran. The stump was on the north bank of the river Skell. The privations of the first months of settlement under the elm tree proved too great for Gervase and Radulf and they left the community to return to York, much to the disgust of their companions. In their place, however, another of the York monks, Adam, who like Robert had previously been a monk at Whitby, joined the Fountains community. Gervase later reappears at Fountains and it is uncertain whether he returned or that Serlo had simply confused him with another monk. Given that he was to lead the first colony from Fountains the latter is more likely.

Abbot Bernard of Clairvaux's reply to the Fountains community can be dated by its contents, for he said that he had heard of the community from his brothers William and Geoffrey. William must be the abbot of Rievaulx attending his first General Chapter at Cîteaux in 1133, and it has been suggested that Geoffrey was Geoffroi d'Ainai, a monk of Clairvaux who may have been present at the setting out of Rievaulx Abbey in 1131–2. Bernard acceded to the convent's request and Geoffroi d'Ainai was dispatched to Fountains, arriving late in 1133. As a monk of advanced years, skilled in Cistercian manners and particularly experienced in the instruction of communities who wished to convert to Cistercian ways, his task was to instruct the Fountains community in the order's philosophy and to provide them with a proper framework within which they could work and pray. Serlo tells us that under Geoffroi's instruction the Fountains monks built 'huts and offices'. This bald statement

4 *Excavation has revealed traces of the first timber buildings to be built in 1133, visible only as the settings of timber posts beneath the foundations of the first stone church. They would have been considerably more sophisticated than the archaeological evidence suggests, and would have required a large amount of timber for their construction. The structures were built in the northern tradition, with ground-cills running between the principal posts, and set in these would have been interlocking wooden staves. The roofs must have been of thatch or shingle for they have left no trace in the ground.*

conceals the truth, for what was provided was a new timber monastery built to the model already provided at Clairvaux, and on a new site. According to the statutes of the order, this would comprise an oratory, a dormitory, a refectory, a chamber for guests and a porter's lodge, the most basic provision necessary for monastic life. No cloister was included and these buildings were intended to serve only until the community achieved stability and could afford to build permanent buildings in stone.

The timber monastery

The move to a new site effected a symbolic break with the Benedictine past, and followed a common Cistercian practice. The new site chosen at Fountains lies at the heart of the surviving ruins and excavation in 1980 revealed parts of two of its timber buildings below the south transept of the standing church. Though many of these buildings are described in Cistercian chronicles and later sources, for instance at Clairvaux itself, at Foigny, at Rievaulx and at Meaux (a later daughter-house of Fountains), physical evidence for these structures is extremely rare. The Fountains buildings are fragmentary, in part destroyed by the construction of later stone buildings on the same site (**4**), but they tell us a great deal about Geoffroi and his instructions. Only the holes dug to take the principal posts of the walls have survived but many of the timbers they had contained had been sawn off at ground level when the buildings were taken down, allowing the stubs to rot

19

away leaving a ghost of their shape in the ground. These ghosts could be measured; they were squared posts 0.40m (1ft 4in) across, set in straight lines, which indicated that the buildings were sophisticated, employing advanced carpentry (**5**). Indeed, Serlo has recorded for us the presence of carpenters and other workmen on site after the harvest of 1133, and they must have been responsible for the excavated buildings. Although the historian Oderic Vital records that the Cistercians 'have built their monasteries with their own labour' the evidence from Fountains is that they can have done little more than clear the site and provide unskilled labour.

The two structures excavated can be identified as the core buildings of the reformed monastery (**6**): the church or oratory which lay east to west, and a domestic building that lay north to south. Four bays of the church survived, 4.9m (16ft 1in) wide and at least 7.6m (24ft 11in) long, though both the east and west ends had been destroyed. Opposed doors were provided in the north and south walls in the westernmost surviving bay, with the door posts being set in pits outside the wall-lines suggesting shallow porches copying a masonry prototype. No internal fittings survived, though given the simplicity of the building the choir stalls may have simply been movable benches. The domestic building appears to have been two-storeyed, although the only evidence for this is deeper post-pits.

The evidence of Clairvaux is critical here, for seventeenth-century descriptions portray the domestic building of the timber monastery in some detail. It was a two-storey building, some

```
0          10          20 FEET
|━━━━━━━━━|━━━━━━━━━|
0          3          6 METRES
|━━━━|━━━━|━━━━|
```

5 *The post-holes of the timber church belie the sophisticated nature of stave-built buildings* (after Herrnbrodt at der Husterknupp).

15m (50ft) long, and lay in a similar position to the fragmentary building at Fountains. Its first floor was the monks' dormitory, and the ground floor was their refectory. There was a small detached kitchen nearby. Given that Geoffroi d'Ainai was responsible for laying out (if not the building of) the timber monastery of Fountains, it seems likely that he would have followed the layout of Clairvaux, his own home, closely. It is interesting to note that Fountains did not subsequently use the Clairvaux layout for the temporary buildings of its own daughter-houses. The only documented example is at Meaux Abbey where Abbot Adam, one of the founding community at Fountains instructed by Geoffroi in 1133, chose to place the oratory over the dormitory in late 1150. Adam was one of two Fountains monks charged with the setting up of daughter-houses, acting in their turn as Geoffroi d'Ainai had before. This change of layout may of course simply reflect a change in Cistercian planning of temporary buildings in line with the order's developing concept of architecture. Indeed, the unknown temporary buildings of Newminster, Woburn and Kirkstall Abbeys, all daughter-houses of Fountains, are recorded as being built 'after the manner of our order'.

Apart from Fountains, the only other site to produce any tangible evidence for the buildings that were to serve as the monastery whilst the convent struggled to become viable is Bordesley Abbey, where early burials were covered with timbers taken from the buildings that had served the community as its first home. Such was the significance of these buildings to the earliest monks that they took them to the grave. Although fragments of the buildings survive, excavation has yet to reveal their location on the site or their plan. When the temporary structures were replaced with stone buildings at Signy Abbey in the Ardennes, any timbers not reused in the new buildings were ceremonially buried within the precinct, such was their symbolic importance.

The threat of failure

The years 1133 and 1134 were a hard time for the Fountains community. Thurstan had only provided a minimal endowment of two carucates (about 105ha or 260 acres) at nearby Sutton and 81ha (200 acres) of the wood of Herleshowe to support the convent, compared with the seven carucates provided by Walter

6 *The post-pits of the first timber church at Fountains (on the left of the plan) show the precise location of the timber wall-posts and double posts (541, 531, and 521) that mark the porches. Cross-hatching shows areas where later building has destroyed the evidence for these earliest buildings.*

Espec at the founding of Rievaulx Abbey which had to support a community of the same size. Rievaulx, being the first Cistercian house to be established in the north of England, immediately attracted other endowments as local landowners sought to share in the spirituality of the men Serlo described as 'speaking on earth with the tongues of angels and who were most worthy of the name of monk'. Fountains following behind simply did not benefit from the same charity and failed to receive the support that would ensure *stabilitas*, the econo-

mic state required before the monastery could formally be accepted into the order. Not only did Fountains fail to attract gifts of land, it also failed to attract the recruits who flocked to Rievaulx. In the short term, this was perhaps as well, for the harvest failed in 1133 whilst the temporary buildings were under construction, reducing the monks to a diet of gruel made from the leaves of their elm tree and field herbs. When Eustace FitzJohn of Knaresborough Castle sent a supply of bread to sustain the community who were on the verge of starvation, its remains were shared between the convent's workmen and the 'starving beggar at the gate'.

By 1134, it was apparent even to the founding community that their efforts must fail, and Abbot Richard went to the General Chapter at Cîteaux with a request to Abbot Bernard of Clairvaux that the community be allowed to abandon Fountains. Bernard reluctantly agreed to the request, and set aside his abbey's

7 *Early estates were all to be found within 10 km (6 miles) of the monastery.*

grange of Longué in the Haute Marne as a new home for the community.

On his return from Burgundy, Abbot Richard was to discover that the situation at Fountains had changed radically for the better, no doubt the result of Archbishop Thurstan's influence as founder. Hugh, the Dean of Thurstan's cathedral church and two more of its canons, another Serlo and Tosti, had chosen to retire to Fountains. All three, and particularly Hugh, were wealthy and brought their wealth and respectability with them. Additionally, Hugh brought his fine library to Fountains. The situation was saved, and the wealth brought by the three canons of York Minster was put to the use of the convent. It was divided into three parts: the first was reserved in true Cistercian spirit for the poor; the second to establish a building fund; and the third part provided for the immediate needs of the community. Once the future appeared secure, endowments of land began to be offered. Robert de Sartis gave three carucates of land of the vill of Herleshow to the south of the abbey and Serlo de Pembroke, a kinsman of Eustace FitzJohn who had provided bread during the famine of 1133, gave two carucates of land at nearby Cayton. Further small estates were given at Aldburgh and Warsill (7), the start of a process that was rapidly to gain momentum throughout the middle years of the twelfth century.

Security allowed the growth of the community, and by October 1135 when Abbot Richard successfully applied to the General Chapter for formal admission into the order he presided over a convent of 35 monks. Fountains was now an equal to Rievaulx Abbey, a daughter-house of Clairvaux charged with forwarding the Cistercian mission in England. With *stabilitas*, the time had come to build a permanent stone monastery, just as it had 29 years previously at Cîteaux.

The first stone monastery

The remarkable change of fortune that befell the Fountains community in 1135 marked the start of a period of sustained spiritual growth and financial security that was to continue well into the thirteenth century. Before his death in 1139, Abbot Richard was to see his convent established in a new stone church which was begun in 1136, one of the earliest known of the order's churches and built within a decade of the writing of Bernard of Clairvaux's *Apologia ad Guilielmum*. Its plan has been partially recovered by excavation and it represents the earliest form of stone church approved by so centralized an order.

Its building marks the second stage in the abbey's life, that of mission-centre responsible for spreading the Cistercian reform throughout England and further afield. The method by which the reform was spread was to dispatch groups of 12 monks and an abbot to establish daughter-houses or colonies on land given by patrons for that purpose. The abbot of each new daughter-house would normally be one of the most senior monks, and in the case of Fountains this meant members of the founding community trained by Geoffroi d'Ainai. The ability to establish colonies was strictly controlled by the availability of monks and the availability of willing patrons, and the events of the late 1130s demonstrate that Fountains' growing reputation attracted both many recruits to the cloister and men of substance who were sufficiently impressed to endow new monasteries. In this, Fountains was to outshine Rievaulx.

The first colonies

The first daughter-house established from Fountains in 1138 was settled on the fen edge

8 *The daughter-houses of Fountains and other members of the filiation in England and Lysa in Norway.*

in Lincolnshire at Haverholme near Sleaford (**8**). The first abbot was Gervase, one of the founding monks from York. A party of lay brothers had been sent to Haverholme the previous year to prepare the site, evidence that Fountains had begun to recruit the *conversi* who were to establish the agricultural fortunes of the house, as well as choir-monks. The site was provided by Alexander 'the Magnificent', the Bishop of Lincoln, a certain sign that the community in Skelldale had achieved spiritual respectability. Alexander had almost certainly been introduced to the Fountains community by Archbishop Thurstan and he was to remain a committed supporter of the Cistercians in his immense diocese that extended from the Thames to the Humber. It appears that this first daughter-house was founded more from piety than practicality and the site proved to be unsuitable, a common problem with many Cistercian colonies, and Bishop Alexander moved the community to a new site in his deer-park at Louth from which the new abbey became known as *de Parco Ludo* or Louth Park.

A second colony was dispatched to the wilds of Northumberland under the abbacy of Robert, the ex-Whitby monk who was one of the first Fountains community. The name given to this daughter-house is significant for it was called *Novum Monasterium* or Newminster, the original name of Cîteaux itself. Its temporary buildings were laid out by Abbot Robert 'after our manner' though the founder, Ranulph de Merlay, Lord of Morpeth, claimed responsibility for their construction. This split responsibility was to ensure that suitable buildings were completed before the new colony arrived, a requirement of Cistercian statutes since at least 1113.

The planning of new colonies took some time, as the foundation of the third daughter-house, of Kirkstead in Lincolnshire, proves. Hugh Brito, the Lord of Tattershall, had visited Fountains in 1137 but two years were spent in preparing the site before Robert de Subella and 12 monks were sent out to settle it. Not only were buildings and monks required for a new foundation, but the statutes of the order required that each new colony was to be sent out with its complement of necessary and officially approved books: a missal, the gospels, a gradual, an antiphonary, a hymnal, a psalter, a copy of the rule and a religious calendar. Because these books had to reflect the Cistercian reform they would have to be copied at the mother-house, a lengthy process in itself. Since the initial foundation of Fountains itself had been so uncertain, careful planning seems generally to have gone hand-in-hand with religious zeal for not one of the eight colonies established from Fountains before 1150 was to fail.

By the death of Abbot Richard, the establishment of daughter-houses had depleted the Fountains community of a quarter of its original members, 36 choir-monks who had joined the first community, and an unknown number of lay brothers. In the same period, Rievaulx, Fountains' natural rival, had only established two colonies, both in 1136. In both cases there appears to have been a direct correlation between the number of recruits to the mother-house and the need to establish colonies, as though the intention was to keep the mother-house to a manageable size. This is reflected at Fountains in the stone church built by Abbot Richard.

A stone church

The earliest stone churches of the Cistercians, those of Cîteaux and Pontigny, known only from contemporary descriptions, were rectangular buildings of great simplicity, a far cry from the monumental cruciform church begun at Clairvaux in 1135 by the architects Achard and Geoffroi d'Ainai and which is now seen as the model for the order's twelfth-century churches. The contemporary church built at Fountains is more typical of the order's early churches, cruciform but with an unstressed crossing, a short square-ended presbytery to house the altar, and small rectangular transept chapels. Only the south transept and parts of the crossing and presbytery have been excavated, but sufficient has been seen to indicate its likely plan (**9** and see **4**).

The new church envelops the site of the timber oratory, an unusual feature, for its building must have interfered with the constant round of services. Normally, a replacement church would have been built on an adjacent site to avoid this inconvenience, but at Fountains the site of the community's first Cistercian church was deemed to be so important that it was to be reused by succeeding churches. More remarkable than the placing of this church, though, was its scale. It was small, and unlike its successors had a short nave without aisles, and the transepts were mere adjuncts, walled off from the main body of the church. It was not built for a large community and must simply have been intended to serve only for the mission phase of the house when numbers of choir monks can have been no greater than 40 or 50. Even so, the church must have seemed distinctly cramped. The lack of a large aisled nave precludes the army of lay brothers that became a feature of the house.

9 *The first stone church survives only as foundations, for its materials were later reused to build its successor. Only the south transept and a part of the crossing have been excavated.*

10 *A reconstruction of the ground-plan of the first stone church at Fountains compared with the undeveloped churches of Waverley, Tintern and Lysa.*

The plan of the church is comparable with the other early churches known at Waverley in Surrey, a grand-daughter of Cîteaux founded in 1128 and built presumably in the early 1130s, and Tintern, founded from Waverley in 1131 (**10**). Nothing survives of the superstructure of the Fountains church but comparison with surviving fabric at Waverley shows that the building was tall and apparently reflected the architecture of the Burgundian cradle of the order. Some indication of the height of the transepts at Fountains can be gained from later buildings that abutted them (**11**). Whilst it respected the Cistercian philosophy of simplicity, the inspiration for the plan can have come from non-Cistercian sources, particularly the simple churches of the Augustinian canons who had spread throughout England a generation before the Cistercians arrived. Similar form and scale can be detected at Portchester Priory, built with royal patronage in the years after 1133, the simple church of Kirkham Priory built in the 1120s, or the Benedictine priory church of Ewenny built in the 1130s but not colonized before 1141.

The Fountains church tells us a great deal about the community that built it. First, it was a free-standing structure without an associated cloister, with a timber domestic building to its south that replaced the earlier timber range.

WAVERLEY (after 1128)   TINTERN (after 1131)   FOUNTAINS (after 1135)   LYSA (after 1146)

60   40ft   60

0

11 *The cloister buildings and nave added to the first stone church by Abbot Henry Murdac before the fire of 1146 can be reconstructed with a fair degree of accuracy. Shown in broken line are extensions to the east and west ranges built during the post-fire reconstruction.*

Secondly, it betrays evidence of the community's Benedictine origins, both in plan and decoration. The east end of the building was built to a stepped plan, with the inner transept chapels being deeper than the outer ones. Although the chapels and presbytery are square-ended in the Cistercian fashion, their plan repeats the stepped apses that marked the east end of York Abbey, perhaps an unconscious repetition of the design of the church the monks had previously known. Like York Abbey, the church had been plastered and painted internally and externally. Most of this plaster was white-limed and overpainted with a masonry pattern common to all orders in the twelfth century. A respond capital had survived and been reset in the lower walling of the later church. This retained traces of multi-coloured leaf decoration that was very un-Cistercian in its appearance. Glass, too, survived from the windows of the south transept chapels, and this was not the plain glass favoured by the order and mandatory from 1147 but included red and blue quarries that implied decorative windows. The simplicity of the order was expressed in other ways. The altars in the transept chapels were simple affairs built of wood, set in the plain mortar floors of the chapels. The main body of the transept had an earth floor, while the more important areas of the choir and presbytery had mortar floors, separated by a single step that marked the entrance to the presbytery. The choir stalls, of which no trace remained, were set against the walls that closed off the transepts, and between them the floor was strewn with compressed layers of rushes.

Abbot Richard was replaced by his prior, another Richard who had been the sacrist at York, a saintly man who felt himself to be unworthy of his promotion and shrank from the administrative duties of the office. He was deeply respected by the community for his religious conviction and ability to resolve spiritual problems but he was not the person to

12 *The ground-plan of a typical Benedictine monastery of the first half of the twelfth century differed little from that of the St Gall plan of the ninth century. The living accommodation of the monks was placed around a square cloister with the church on the north side. The dormitory occupied the first floor of the east range above the chapter-house, parlour and dayroom, and the abbot's house occupied the first floor of the west range above the outer parlour and cellarage. (Compare with **14A**.)*

involve himself with great building schemes, and between 1139 and his death in 1143 Fountains enjoyed a period of consolidation. During his abbacy, Archbishop Thurstan died, depriving the community of its principal patron, and Richard II involved the abbey in a dispute over his successor that was to have disastrous consequences in later years (see p.32–3).

In 1144, Abbot Bernard of Clairvaux intervened in the affairs of Fountains to provide a strong leader who would impress Cistercian orthodoxy on the convent which still retained traces of its Benedictine past, Henry Murdac, Abbot of Vauclair, was sent to Fountains ostensibly to advise the community on the choice of a new abbot but in reality to be elected himself. A Yorkshireman and Master of the Schools in York, he had taught Abbot William of Rievaulx before both had entered Clairvaux.

Henry became a close friend of Bernard, and Clairvaux-trained and a zealot forceful to the point of being overbearing, he was just the person to ensure the strengthening of the abbey, being the first abbot trained in continental European practice. Murdac was a builder, he had seen the rebuilding of the church and cloister at Clairvaux, and as abbot of Vauclair had been responsible for building the church there on the Clairvaux model. At Fountains he was to complete the building of the first stone monastery, and was indirectly responsible for its destruction by fire in 1146.

Abbot Henry Murdac's buildings
Murdac must have been appalled by what he found at Fountains on his arrival in 1144. The small stone church and timber domestic build-

13 *Part of Murdac's east cloister range survives to full height encased within a later rebuilding. It can be identified by its small, roughly-squared blocks of gritstone with wide mortar joints, the remains of thick external white-limed plaster, and with absolutely plain doors and windows detailed in good quality ashlar.*

ings represented an outdated philosophy, for the Cistercians had moved back to the principles of un-reformed Benedictine planning that had been abandoned by the founding generation. The reason for this was simply growing numbers and the success of the reform movement. The order had taken the standard Benedictine layout (**12**) and modified it to their own needs and taste. Gone was the informal layout of simple buildings, to be replaced by the formal enclosure of the cloister. The presence of lay brothers required a departure from the Benedictine plan, for their accommodation was to be separate from that of the choir monks and they were to have their own church. Their presence also required the provision of an Outer Court within the monastery where they could work,

separated again from the monks, to emphasize their secondary status.

Murdac's primary task was therefore to enlarge the first stone church and build permanent cloister buildings of the latest continental Cistercian design for the community. The first thing that is apparent about Murdac's building is its scale. A vast cloister was laid out to the south of the existing church, 38m (125ft) square, contemporary with the addition of a great aisled nave to Abbot Richard's small church. This cloister survives today. Considerable parts of Murdac's cloister ranges, the house he built for the community, also still survive, embedded in later buildings. Enough remains above ground or has been excavated over the past 22 years to reconstruct not only the plan of his monastery but also to recover details of its elevations (see **11**). His buildings, which were completed in less than three years, can be recognized by their distinctive masonry (**13** and see **95**). Parts of the east, south and west cloister ranges survive to their full height of 6.10m (20ft), capped by a chamfered string-course that carried the eaves of the roof. Excavation has demonstrated that all the buildings

wall extant or excavated
wall surmised
wall re-used
post fire extension

14 *The ground plan of Abbot Henry's monastery (A) has been identified by a study of its surviving remains and by excavation. Its buildings remain within the monastery that was reconstructed in the later twelfth century (B).*

were roofed in tile. The ranges were 7m (23ft) wide internally, the same width as the earliest cloister ranges recently identified at Rievaulx, a fact that might suggest modular planning that has already been identified in early Cistercian churches. These new and closely dated cloister buildings provide the finest example of early twelfth-century planning in the order (**14A** and see **11**) and demonstrate the best continental practice that must have been derived from Clairvaux itself, where the early twelfth-century buildings have largely been destroyed.

Before any building could be contemplated, the river Skell was moved some 26m (84ft) to the south and a stone-lined drain was constructed along its old line to flush latrines that were to be built to serve both the lay brothers in the west range and the choir-monks in the east range. Next, a terrace was created on the valley floor approximately level with the floor of Abbot Richard's church. On this terrace the new cloister buildings were raised. The east range was butted up to the south transept of the existing stone church, but the contemporary west range

was bonded with the south wall of the extended nave, showing that it must also be the work of Abbot Henry.

The east range was of two storeys and still survives at its south end to full height. Against the south transept of the church was the chapter-house where the abbey's business was conducted, discipline enforced and a daily chapter of the Rule of St Benedict heard. It was contained within the range and must have been a low, dark room for its ceiling was the wooden floor of the dormitory above that was only 2.14m (7ft) above ground level. To the south of the chapter-house was the parlour, the only room in which conversation was allowed. Next came the day-stair to the dormitory, approached by a tall door now blocked from the cloister. The stair itself must have been of timber for it has left no trace, but a small room below the stair was lit by a round-headed window in the east wall which still survives (see **95**). To the south of the day-stair was a passage through the range, and to the south of this the day-room set aside for manual work within the cloister. In a Benedictine monastery this room would have been provided with fireplaces and doubled as the warming-house where fires were permitted between 1 November and Good Friday, but at Fountains there is no evidence that this room was heated at all, a certain indication that Cistercian life was meant to be hard and unremitting.

To the east of the east range was a long building partially set over the original course of the Skell. Its upper floor was the monks' latrine, communicating with their dormitory by a door which still survives and to the north of which is the round-headed opening in which a lamp was placed to light access to the latrines at night. Its ground floor had a long, narrow room walled off from the latrine drain, traditionally set aside for the training of novices. Latrine chutes in the thickness of its south wall show that the monks' latrine also served a yard between it and the Skell, an area set aside for manual work outside the cloister. All monasteries took sanitation seriously, but none more so than the Cistercians who were particularly conspicuous for the attention they paid to drainage. This latrine block was set over a massive drain laid in the original bed of the river Skell that was continually flushed by water from the river, ensuring that the site was kept free of sewage and the risk of disease that it carried.

The upper floor of the east range, the monks' dorter or dormitory, was lit by a series of small round-headed windows and was an undivided space 49m (160ft) long. The monks' beds would have been ranged along the side walls, allowing space for approximately 80 choir-monks. Night access to the church was provided by a door in the gable wall of the south transept, but the principal access was by the day-stair from the east cloister alley.

The ground-floor refectory, aligned west to east, was open to the roof in the same manner as a domestic hall. At the east end of the range a passage runs through the range at ground-floor level, leading to a yard on the south side of the refectory, and there was a room above the passage accessible from the monks' dormitory. This may be a private chamber for the abbot who lived in common with his monks and was required by statute to sleep within the dormitory.

The west range was the home of the lay brothers and with the exception of the chapter-house it mirrored the accommodation provided for the monks, providing an open dormitory 64m (210ft) long at first-floor level, large enough to house perhaps 140 lay brothers. At the north end of the ground floor was the outer parlour where monks and lay brethren alike could receive visitors from the outside world. Towards the centre was cellarage which extended almost the full length of the cloister. South of this was a passage through the range flanked by a porter's lodge which provided access to the cloister alleys. Immediately to the south of this, the remainder of the range was taken up by the lay brothers' refectory. An offset visible on the inner face of the east wall shows that the ground floor, like that of the east range, was only 2.10m (7ft) high. The lay brothers' latrine, still unexcavated, lay above the old course of the Skell to the west of the range. The east and west ranges extended to within 6m (20ft) of the north bank of the realigned river and in the yard between them would have been a detached kitchen, probably served by a bridge across the Skell. A metalled path has been located, skirting the south end of the west range and leading into the kitchen yard.

Of Murdac's enlargement of the church only a short length of its south nave wall can be seen. From this it appears that aisles were added to the earlier nave which was extended substantially to the west. The purpose was to provide a church for the lay brothers in the nave. Aisles were necessary as passages to provide access since the main body of the church was divided into liturgical units by screens. To establish the likely plan of Murdac's nave it is necessary to look at the church he built at Vauclair before he came to Fountains, for the nave of the early church at Fountains has yet to be excavated.

The abbey of Vauclair was founded in 1134 and permanent buildings were begun within a year or two of settlement and it is likely that construction of the church was completed before Murdac's departure for Fountains in 1144. Abbot Henry's church was unknown before its excavation in the late 1960s (15). Only the foundations had survived a later rebuilding but the plan they demonstrate is the earliest known example of 'Bernardine' planning derived from the great church of Clairvaux itself. The two churches must in fact be closely contemporary in date. The nave of nine bays is what concerns us here, for its dimensions bear a remarkably close resemblance to the dimensions of Murdac's nave at Fountains which must have been closely modelled on it. Its appearance is unknown but another contemporary church, that of the Clairvaux colony of Fontenay, remains intact. Built between 1139 and 1147 it is closely contemporary with

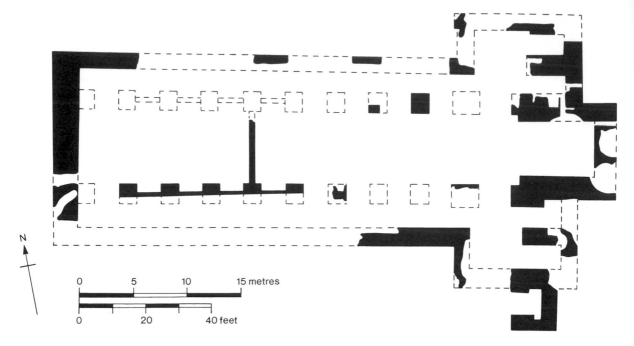

N

0   5   10   15 metres

0   20   40 feet

15 *Ground-plan of Henry Murdac's church at
Vauclair, one of the earliest known great
churches of the family of Clairvaux, built
shortly before he became abbot of Fountains in
1144* (after Courtois).

Murdac's churches and its stark Burgundian
detailing (**16**) with pointed arches to the main
arcades might give a clue as to the appearance
of the Fountains nave. Unlike Fontenay, Fountains appears to have had an upper storey
lighting its nave, and it would have been roofed
in timber. This was the model favoured at
Clairvaux and the lack of a clerestory at Fontenay may simply be a mark of lower status
within the order.

The destruction of Fountains in 1146
Abbot Richard II had involved his abbey in the
disputed election of William FitzHerbert to the
archbishopric of York in 1140. King Stephen
had nominated William to the see against the
united opposition of the Augustinians and Cistercians who did not consider him to be a
suitable candidate. Abbot Richard II, supported
by Bernard of Clairvaux, took the case to Rome
and persuaded Pope Eugenius III, himself a
Cistercian monk, to withhold recognition of the
election. Richard himself died at Clairvaux
and his successor, Abbot Henry, no doubt

instructed by St Bernard, took up the fight with
his customary zeal. Henry himself soon became
the favoured candidate of the opposition party,
bringing accusations of simony against the
archbishop at the Council of Rheims that were
to lead to his deposition early in 1147.

So intense was the antagonism in 1146 that
supporters of Archbishop William marched on
Fountains seeking to murder Abbot Henry.
Unable to find him, they sacked the abbey,
finding little of value in the process, and fired
its buildings. Serlo, who was present during the
attack, tells how 'the convent stood by and saw
the buildings erected by the sweat of their
brows enveloped in flames and soon to be ashes,
and that only the oratory and offices adjoining
it reserved for prayer remained half-consumed,
like a branch plucked from the burning', a
slight exaggeration to judge from what survives. Excavation has proved, however, that
his overall description of the event was
reasonably accurate. Traces of a serious fire
have been found in both the east and west
cloister ranges and in the south transept of the
church itself (**17**), where the burning was sufficiently severe to melt the window glass and
bring down the wall-plaster. Henry Murdac
himself had been in the church during the
assault, prostrated before the high altar, and it
is significant that no trace of burning was
found in the area of the choir and presbytery,

16 The abbey church of Fontenay built between 1139 and 1147 and closely contemporary with the first stone church at Fountains, remains complete, demonstrating the simplicity of the 'Bernardine' model (Terryl Kinder).

17 Intense burning in the southern chapel of the south transept left melted window glass and fallen wall-plaster fused to the floor.

where the rushes on the floor were not even charred. The wall that separated the transept from the crossing had evidently contained the fire, and miraculously the abbey church survived in a usable state.

FitzHerbert's deposition in 1147 left the way clear for Abbot Henry's election to the archbishopric, though King Stephen refused to invest him with the temporalities of the see and feeling ran so strongly against him that he was unable to enter his own cathedral city. It was a pyrrhic victory that had cost his convent their home and forced him to administer his archdiocese from the bishops' palace in Ripon that the founding community had left with such hopes on 27 December 1132.

Reconstruction

Henry Murdac was obliged to resign his abbacy when he became archbishop, though he continued to impose his will on two of his successors. The first was Maurice, who had previously been the second abbot of Rievaulx and before he joined the Cistercians there, had been subprior of the great Benedictine cathedral-priory of Durham. After only three months he retired again to Rievaulx, finding his position intolerable, to be succeeded by another Rievaulx monk, Thorold, who was later to become abbot of Trois-Fontaines. To Thorold fell the task of rebuilding the ruined abbey. In Serlo's words, the monks 'repaired the fallen places and rebuilt the ruins, and as it was written "the walls had fallen but were rebuilt with squared stones"'. The south transept of the church was refitted, with new mortar floors and stone altars in the eastern chapels which sealed the evidence of burning (**18**). The cloister ranges must have been left roofless shells, and a grant of timber by Alan, Earl of Richmond, in 1147 might be associated with the replacement of burned floors and roofs. It is impossible to tell from what remains if more drastic reconstruction was required. The opportunity was taken during the post-fire repair to extend both the west and east ranges to the north bank of the Skell (both extensions are shown on **11** in broken line), extending both the lay brothers' and monks' dormitories to allow for growing numbers as well as providing additional room

18 *A new stone altar set on a mortar floor replaced the timber altar in the southern transept chapel destroyed by fire in 1146.*

at ground-floor level. The replacement of the wooden floor to the lay brothers' dormitory with a stone vault supported on masonry piers had the effect of fire-proofing the ground floor.

The second phase of colonization
Abbot Henry continued the policy of missionary colonization begun by Abbot Richard when he persuaded Hugh de Bolbec to endow a daughter-house at Woburn in Bedfordshire in 1145 (see **8**). The colony was lead by Alan, one of the founding group at Fountains, and additionally brother Adam was again employed to set out the temporary buildings. Adam's future career suggests that he may indeed have been specifically trained by Geoffroi d'Ainai to set out the Fountains family of monasteries, though we have no idea what his contribution to the building of the first stone monastery at Fountains itself was.

Following the destruction of Fountains by FitzHerbert's supporters, three more daughter-houses were settled in 1146–7, the number suggesting the need to reduce the size of the mother-community while repairs were carried out. The first of these in 1146 demonstrated the internationalism of the Cistercians. Led by Ranulf a colony set out for Norway, settling at Lysa near Bergen at the invitation of Bishop Sigurd who had visited Fountains and who provided the site. Clairvaux had already settled a daughter-house at Alvastra in Sweden in 1143, and the settlement of Lysakloster from Fountains suggests a policy within the Clairvaux family to bring the Cistercian mission to Scandinavia, planned by St Bernard himself. In 1147, monks from Kirkstead were settled at Hovedö, and Lysa itself established a daughter-house at Tutterö in 1207, completing the Cistercian settlement of Norway within the Fountains family.

The second colony set out in March to settle at Barnoldswick in Craven under the patronage of two powerful Yorkshire barons, William de Poitou and Henry de Lacy. They were led by Alexander, and the party of 12 monks included Serlo who by this time would have been one of the senior members of the Fountains community. The site at Barnoldswick was not an ideal one, it proved too wet and was based on a pre-existing settlement that did not provide the detachment from the world that the Cistercian statutes required. Abbot Alexander's demolition of the parish church did little to improve relations with the local community, and the convent moved to a better site at Kirkstall in the valley of the Aire to the west of Leeds on the advice of their patrons in 1152. The third colony was led by Warrin, exceptionally not one of the monks from York, and set out for Bytham in Lincolnshire where a site had been granted by William le Gros, Count of Aumale and Earl of Yorkshire. Like Barnoldswick, this site proved unsatisfactory, this time having too little water, and in 1149 the convent moved to a new site provided by one of William's tenants that they called *Vallis Dei*, the Valley of God, and which became known in English as Vaudey. Here the abbey buildings were again laid out by brother Adam. The failure of both initial sites suggests that they were chosen too hurriedly, supporting the suggestion that monks were being removed from Fountains because of the abbey's destruction rather than in a carefully planned policy of colonization.

Planned during the reconstruction of Fountains and settled late in 1150 was an eighth and final colony at Meaux in Holderness. Brother Adam had met William le Gros in 1149 when he was engaged in laying out the buildings of Vaudey and had been asked to advise the count how he could redeem a pledge made in his youth to go on pilgrimage to the Holy Land that he could no longer undertake because he had grown too old and fat. He was already the patron of three monasteries including Vaudey. Brother Adam suggested the foundation of a second Cistercian abbey, and Pope Eugenius III readily agreed to a dispensation. Adam was to lead the colony himself and William invited him to choose a site on his extensive estates. He chose, to the count's distress, the land in Holderness 'well planted with woods and orchards, surrounded with rivers and waters and favoured with rich soil' that William had recently purchased and was in the process of enclosing as a hunting park.

The establishment of Meaux Abbey ended the first generation of the Fountains family. A second generation was also growing, for Newminster under its first abbot, St Robert, had established colonies of its own: at Pipewell in Northamptonshire in 1143; at Roche in south Yorkshire in 1147; and at Sawley in Craven in 1148 (see **8**). In England, the Fountains family was complete and the mission phase was over. From 1150, Fountains Abbey was to be transformed from a missionary outpost to the head of a substantial family of subsidiary abbeys, like Clairvaux a mother-house at the head of its own filiation.

3

Fountains – the mother house

The removal of Abbot Thorold in 1150 marked a watershed in the history of Fountains for it coincided with the end of the mission phase of the house. Urged by Archbishop Henry, St Bernard returned Thorold to Rievaulx for he had proved to be too independent. In his place Bernard imposed an excellent candidate, Richard of Clairvaux, a native of York like Murdac and Abbot William of Rievaulx, and a man of great austerity trained in the best continental Cistercian practice. He had risen to be precentor at Clairvaux and followed Murdac as abbot of Vauclair.

This new Abbot Richard, formally elected in 1151, had the difficult job of keeping the peace with Archbishop Henry until his death in 1153 and arranging a reconciliation with the restored Archbishop William FitzHerbert thereafter. William in his turn became a good friend of Fountains, visiting in May 1154 and promising financial support for building work then in hand. The ending of the 13-year-old dispute in turn allowed Fountains to recover from the disturbed and weakened state the feud had caused, and before the abbot's death in 1170 the Augustinian canon William of Newburgh was to describe Fountains, together with Rievaulx and Byland, as one of the 'three shining lights' of northern monasticism. All three had exceptional abbots at the time who all were great builders.

Recovery and growing numbers no longer relieved by the foundation of daughter-houses resulted in a cramped community, for Murdac's cloister buildings were too small for the numbers of monks and lay brothers who flocked to the abbey. As the head of a good-sized family, Fountains also enjoyed an enhanced status within the order and required rather grander buildings than it possessed to demonstrate this. Abbot Richard III began a campaign of building that was to continue into the last decade of the twelfth century, transforming his abbey from a simple daughter-house of Clairvaux to the mother-house of a substantial *familia* (see **14B**).

A great stone church

First to be built, or at least begun, was a monumental new church (**colour plates 1** and **6**), which was started within a few years of Abbot Richard's election and probably occasioned Archbishop William's visit. Its inspiration came not directly from France but from nearby Rievaulx, where a similar church had been begun by the very English abbot, St Aelred, perhaps five years earlier, for his rapidly growing community. The rebuilding of the church at Fountains was to begin a rivalry of building campaigns that was to last well into the following century. Rivalry was not only expressed in buildings, but also in the religious zeal which drew recruits. Under Aelred, Rievaulx grew to house at least 500 lay brothers and 150 choir-monks. Fountains was never able to achieve numbers like these, for even at their greatest extent its cloister buildings cannot have housed more than 120 monks and 400 lay brethren.

A great deal remains of Aelred's church at Rievaulx (**19**) or was recovered by excavation in the early 1920s. Burgundian in style, it conforms to the 'Bernardine' plan first expressed by the great church at Clairvaux itself. The church at Rievaulx was the first great Cistercian church to be built in England, with an aisled nave of nine bays and a two-storey elevation. Its transepts survive to full height

19 *Abbot Aelred's church at Rievaulx of which the nave and transepts remain provided the model for the new church begun at Fountains by Abbot Richard of Clairvaux.*

and sufficient remains of the nave to be sure of its design (**20A**). Detailing was severe almost to the point of non-existence, the piers and pointed arches of the nave being boldly chamfered but lacking any moulding and rising from plain square bases. The roughly-coursed rubble that made up the walls was plastered, white-limed, and lined out in white paint to resemble good quality masonry. The nave aisles were vaulted transversely, carrying back the profiles of the nave arcades to the side walls, a feature seen at Fontenay (see **16**), designed to support the thrust of a high vault. The nave was not vaulted, however, but roofed in wood. In this Rievaulx belongs to an early group of great Cistercian churches best represented by the church of Clermont (**21**) built in the 1150s.

Though the model for the new church of Fountains was undoubtedly Aelred's church at Rievaulx, its design marked a significant development in Cistercian architecture. Its plan and two-storey elevation were definitely taken from Rievaulx, but its architectural detailing was not. Instead, this was developed separately using details first seen in England at Sawley

Abbey, a grand-daughter house of Fountains begun after 1147, and almost certainly the direct inspiration for the design of Fountains itself.

The church at Fountains, though starkly devoid of decoration, was meant from the first to demonstrate the wealth and importance of the abbey and like the great church at Clairvaux was built to a scale that was out of keeping with the simplicity urged in St Bernard's *Apologia*. In this it went further than the Rievaulx church, for though it was built for a smaller community it was significantly longer, having a nave of 11 bays, and was built throughout of finely cut ashlar masonry, though it was white-limed and painted in the same manner as Rievaulx. Building exclusively in carefully cut masonry, even though the quarry was adjacent to the church, was slow and costly, and it is hardly surprising that Serlo records that it was not completed for some 20 years. He also says, with characteristic understatement, that it rose 'far more lavish' than its small predecessor. The period of its building falls conveniently between Bernard of Clairvaux's death in 1153 and his canonization in 1174.

The new church has a complicated structural history caused partly by its being built around its predecessor so far as was practicable. The

37

A

B

20 *Comparative bay elevations of the naves of (A) Rievaulx (after Harrison) and (B) Fountains (after Reeve).*

reason for this was the constant need for a church to house the altar and in which the community could sing the seven daily offices and celebrate Mass. The first parts to be built were the presbytery, transepts and crossing, requiring the demolition of the same parts of the earlier church. Although Richard of Clairvaux's presbytery was later demolished, his transepts with their eastern chapels remain

virtually intact (**22**). The tall pointed arches into the transept chapels are simply relieved by chamfering and have neither bases nor capitals. Above there is blank walling capped by tall, round-headed windows. The church was intentionally tall and austere, with a distinct Burgundian flavour. Originally, the crossing was designed simply as a continuation of the nave up to the entrance of the presbytery, without a central tower at the intersection.

The nave, which demonstrates a radical change in design, was not built at the same time as the transepts, but shortly after. Presumably Murdac's nave survived in use to

21 *(Above) The nave of the abbey church of Clermont is perhaps the finest surviving example of the 'Bernadine' tradition demonstrated by the ruined nave at Rievaulx (Terryl Kinder).*

house the altar and the monks' choir while the eastern part of the new church was being built. Only when the eastern parts of the new church were substantially complete could it be demolished and a new nave built. A clue to the sequence of events is the door (**23**) leading from the new nave into the east walk of the cloister. It is almost certainly reused from Murdac's nave as is much of the facing stone of the south aisle wall which, particularly on its inner face, is of poorer quality than the ashlar used elsewhere in Abbot Richard's work.

The transept of the new church was linked to the existing east range by a rebuilt section of the range that intruded into the original chapter-house and which contained a library and sacristy on the ground floor with the truncated northern part of the dormitory above. This rebuilding was carried up only to the height of the existing east range. Quite clearly, the intention was only to add a new church to Murdac's cloister buildings at this stage, and this is confirmed by two features in the south transept gable. The first of these is the provision of two windows at clerestory level which

22 *(Below) The earliest surviving work in the church at Fountains is found in the south transept and its eastern chapels.*

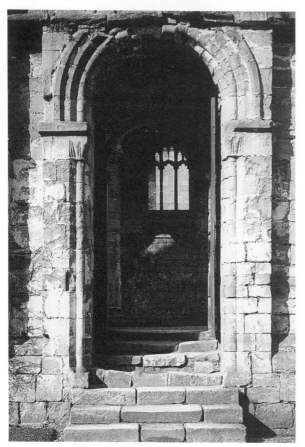

23 *The processional door to the cloister dates to the 1140s and is probably reused from Murdac's church.*

were placed to be clear of the east range roof. The second was the night-stair provided from the new church to the old dormitory. Because the new church was built on a raised terrace 1m (3ft) above its predecessor, the floor of the dormitory was only 1.52m (5ft) above the transept floor. A tall door at floor level was incorporated in the south wall of the transept, through which a short stair provided the necessary access.

When work began on the building of the nave in the late 1150s, provision was made for a central tower. Towers had originally been forbidden by the General Chapter but that proscription had begun to weaken as Cistercian architecture continued to develop. In 1157, the General Chapter amended the statutes to the effect that 'stone towers with bells not be built'. The crossing tower built at Fountains was not a bell-tower but a lantern to throw light into the

choir area, the heart of the church, and it is highly significant that the early Cistercians saw light as a manifestation of the Holy Spirit.

The new nave marked a second stage, therefore, in the design of the great church and it is fortunate that it still survives virtually in the state it was built (**colour plate 5**). It was constructed in sections though it represents a unified design. The eastern four bays which housed the choir-monks' church were the first to be built. They supported the crossing and were presumably closed off at the west end with a temporary timber screen on the line of the later rood screen. The footings of the whole structure must have been laid out when work began, for the next part of the church to be built was the west front and the four western bays that overlapped Murdac's lay brothers' range. The south aisle wall was completed to close off the cloister. Work was then temporarily abandoned, and was not resumed until the 1170s when Abbot Robert of Pipewell completed the church and provided a choir for the lay brothers.

The nave maintained the two-storey elevation of the transepts, and was very clearly modelled on Rievaulx (see **20B**), both in plan and elevation, though it demonstrates a remarkable development in only a few years. The Fountains nave is taller and better proportioned, and the harshness of the Rievaulx design has been lost. Although it is still an austere building, decoration has begun to appear (**24**). Cylindrical piers rose from moulded bases and were capped by scalloped capitals that carried moulded arcades of two orders, and the corbels that carried the transverse arches across the aisles were decorated with fine Anglo-Norman leaf detail. As at Rievaulx, the nave aisles were provided with transverse vaults and the main span had a wooden roof which was boarded in to provide the impression of a vault. The line of this timber ceiling can still be seen in the profile of the arch on the inner face of the west gable (**colour plate 6**) that contains the west window.

The original design of the west front, built about 1160, can be reconstructed. Across the width of the nave are three equal-sized round-headed recesses, the central one framing the main door to the church, while those to either side contained benches in a localized widening of the wall that supported a gallery. Above the gallery were three round-headed windows, and

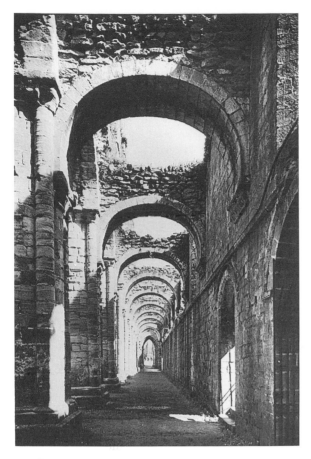

24 *Decoration, unknown at Rievaulx, can be seen in the scalloped and waterleaf capitals of the nave piers and on the corbels that carry the transverse arches of the aisle vaults.*

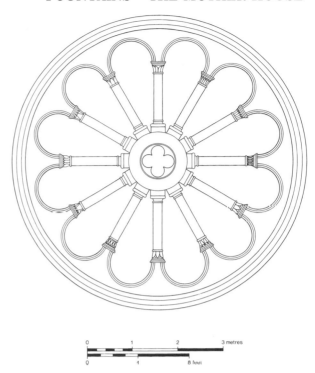

25 *Although the windows of the west gable were taken out at the end of the fifteenth century, substantial fragments of the twelfth-century rose window have been recovered from the west wall of the church. The earliest Cistercian rose window to be recorded in England, it provides the first evidence for the softening of Cistercian ideals* (Stuart Harrison).

above them, filling the space below the ceiling, was a large rose window (**25**). Circular windows were a common feature of Cistercian churches, though few survive today. Associated with the cult of the Virgin, they were particularly appropriate to an order whose churches were invariably dedicated to Her, though they provided an excuse for decoration that was otherwise carefully avoided. The western rose at Fountains is the earliest known example in a Cistercian context.

Externally, the west doors were covered by a porch which was a common feature of early Cistercian churches. It had a central door flanked by open round-headed arcades supported on twin shafts of a design normally associated with cloister arcades (**26**). The detailing of the arcades and the west portal of the nave itself are comparable with the finest contemporary surviving French Cistercian buildings.

It is possible to reconstruct the internal planning of the church from the evidence of sockets cut in the masonry to fix screens and furniture (**27**). Although the nave and transepts are now an uninterrupted space, this was not the case originally and the church was divided into a series of distinct functional compartments. This partitioning shows clearly how a major Cistercian church was used, divided between the two 'churches' of the lay brothers and the choir-monks. The seven western bays of the nave comprised the lay brothers' church and cuts in

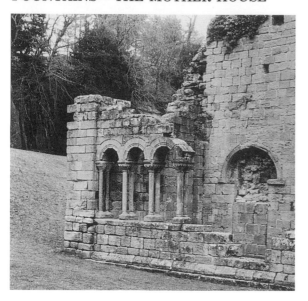

26 *The galilee porch that covered the west doors of the nave was a common feature of great Cistercian churches in the twelfth century. It was a popular burial place for lay patrons whose burial in the church itself was originally discouraged. It was reconstructed from fallen elements in the 1850s.*

27 *The church at Fountains was divided by screens into a series of discrete 'spaces', particularly the distinct churches of the choir-monks and lay brothers, and its barn-like interior was never meant to be seen as one volume (after Fergusson with additions).*

the seventh piers from the west indicate the position of the rood screen against which the nave altar was placed. Between the first and sixth piers of the nave, stone screen walls were provided, against which the lay brothers' choir stalls were placed. The aisles were simply corridors providing access to the eastern parts of the church. Beyond the rood screen the monks' church began. The eighth bay of the nave served as their retrochoir where the old and infirm were allowed to sit during services, in greater comfort than in the choir. The next bay was taken up by the pulpitum, the screen that defined the western extremity of the monks' choir and which contained two chapels, that on the north dedicated to the Virgin and that on the south to St Bernard. Over the chapels was a loft and between them was the lower entrance to the choir. The monks' choir occupied the eastern two bays of the nave and the crossing, their wooden stalls backing up against similar stone walls to those provided in the lay brothers' choir. The upper entrances to the choir were immediately to the east of the eastern crossing piers, and the inner transept chapels were extended to allow for the use of their western bays as vestibules. To the east, a single step defined the sanctuary within the presbytery where the main altar was placed. Nothing is known about the screening of the north transept but it should mirror the arrangement of the south transept which is known in great detail from excavation. Here, a timber screen set in the floor closed off the

40ft

60   60

0

28 *A reconstruction of the church and cloister buildings as they would have appeared at the end of the abbacy of Richard of Clairvaux in 1170 with work unfinished on both the nave of the church and the lay brothers' range.*

transept from the crossing aisle with an entrance at its west end, and tall parclose screens were fitted into the entrances of the central and southern chapels. Further screens in the body of the transept enclosed spaces in front of the chapels.

This great church had a mortar floor throughout, except perhaps for the presbytery east of the step which, by analogy with the contemporary church at Bordesley, might have been paved with stone flags. The only decoration was the painting of the whole building inside and out with limewash over which a masonry pattern was outlined in white paint. No other colour was used. The windows were glazed with pale green glass leaded in geometric or *grisaille* patterns and set in wooden frames, the fixings for which remain in the clerestory windows. Very few traces of the original furnishings of the church survive, but the statutes of the order forbade crosses and candlesticks of precious metal, or set with gems. Wooden altar crosses were preferred, and these might exceptionally be painted. The

church, like the cloister ranges, was roofed not in lead, but with large orange ceramic tiles which were also used to pack up undersized stone blocks in the structure. In all, it represented an exercise in restraint that would have compared starkly with a contemporary Benedictine or Cluniac church, a positive statement of the fundamentalism that the order espoused.

The rebuilding of the cloister
While the church was building, the number of monks and lay brothers was steadily growing and it was not long before Murdac's cloister ranges were uncomfortably full. The only solution was to abandon work on the church in the early 1160s and concentrate instead on enlarging and rebuilding the cloister ranges (**28**). In the meantime, the lay brothers' church in the nave remained incomplete and their services must have been held elsewhere, perhaps in the monks' refectory which was not included in Abbot Richard III's remodelling of the cloister. Because the convent had to be housed and the constant round of services continue during the building operations, the sequence of building became complicated in the extreme. Although this work considerably enlarged the cloister buildings, the plan adopted by Murdac was retained.

The earliest work, which almost certainly belongs to the first years of Richard's abbacy,

43

29 The lay brothers' latrine block, originally built as a freestanding building in the river Skell. To its east is the south end of the lay brothers' range added by Robert of Pipewell in the 1170s.

was a new latrine block for the lay brothers (**29**), placed in the river Skell to the south and west of their original range. It was planned as a freestanding building with latrines at both ground-floor and first-floor level. A blocked door in the north wall at first-floor level is an original feature, showing that the latrine block was entered by a wooden bridge across the river that led to a two-storey timber-framed building on the north bank. This must have been built to serve as a temporary home for the lay brothers while their range was being rebuilt. Murdac's west range was demolished to ground level with the exception of its east wall which was retained to ensure the enclosure of the cloister, and a new range was laid out that was wider, longer and higher than its predecessor. Its building was to prove a lengthy affair and the lay brothers must have occupied their temporary quarters for a decade or more.

The foundations of the range, including the four tunnels that were to carry it over the Skell and connect it to the latrine block, were laid out in the early 1160s, and walling was carried up to just below window cill level. The new range was almost twice the size of its predecessor,

13m (42ft) wide and 91.5m (300ft) long, of 22 double bays. The dormitory at first-floor level could have easily accommodated 400 lay brothers. At first, only the northern 13 bays were completed in the same late Norman style adopted for the church and a temporary blocking wall was built to close off its south end, allowing the range to be used, most probably by the choir-monks whose own range was the next to be rebuilt. Widening the range required alterations to the church, showing that the rebuilding was not considered when the nave was designed. At the south end of the completed northern half of the range a small building was provided against the west wall beneath the day-stairs to the lay brothers' dormitory. This was an office for the cellarer whose stores were housed in the ground floor of the range to the south of the outer parlour. From here to the new door in the south aisle wall ran an arcade with a pent roof that was to serve as the lay brothers' cloister.

Next, attention turned to the rebuilding of the monks' accommodation in the east range where the work was less substantial but equally impressive. The southern part of the original range was retained, its windows and doors blocked up and new masonry added to raise the height of the range substantially (**30**). The groove cut to take the lead flashing of the higher roof can still be seen cutting across the windows of the south transept gable. As well as

30 *The rebuilt monks' dormitory range incorporates in its lower walling the greater part of the pre-fire range. The southern end of the range comprised the dayroom. A central row of pillars originally supported a groined vault on which the floor of the monks' dormitory was carried.*

raising the height of the range, it was extended at its south end where a new latrine block was built on the north bank of the river, enabling the drain to be flushed directly by the Skell, an improvement on its predecessor which was too small for the growing community.

The ground floor of the range was extensively replanned. To the south of the library and sacristy at the north end of the range a new chapter-house, one of the largest ever built in England, was inserted, extending well to the east like St Aelred's chapter-house at Rievaulx, but of a very different plan. Aelred had adapted the Benedictine form with an apsidal east end,

but at Fountains a square end was provided. Entered from the east cloister alley by three richly moulded doors of equal height, the room was divided into three aisles of six bays by tall, monolithic columns that supported a vaulted ceiling (**31**). The two western bays within the range served as a vestibule and were vaulted at a lower level to allow the dormitory above to continue uninterrupted. The two lateral doors from the cloister led not into this vestibule but into a pair of timber-screened book-cupboards, showing that the library had been moved from its original location. The chapter-house was second only in importance to the church for it was here that the corporate life of the monastery was conducted, duties allocated, faults confessed and punishment decreed. It was also the burial place of abbots, and Richard of Clairvaux, the first abbot to be buried at Fountains, was interred here in 1170, his grave being set centrally between the two eastern piers at the foot of the abbot's chair. His burial in what must have been a completed building provides a convenient date for the completion of work to the whole of the range. Unlike the church, the chapter-house was, by Cistercian standards at least, a highly-decorated building, though the two structures are broadly contemporary. Where the church is massive and romanesque, the chapter-house is light, finely proportioned and gothic in its inspiration. The piers that supported the vault were of grey Nidderdale 'marble' (its earliest use at Fountains) that contrasted with the white paintwork of the walls and ceiling, the capitals and corbels had fine leaf decoration and the vault had moulded ribs. A similar contrast can be seen at Rievaulx and at Fontenay, and it would appear that architectural forms were adapted to function and that austerity was not necessarily all pervading.

At the same time as the chapter-house was being built, the parlour to the south was remodelled. It had a cloister door matching the entrance to the chapter-house and a new door in its east wall leading to an enclosed yard beyond the range and was bounded by the new chapter-house and latrine block. It had a rib vault of three bays supported on triple corbels carved with unusual and severely beautiful leaf designs. Decoration was beginning to become accepted.

The southern half of the range was vaulted in seven double bays from a central row of piers

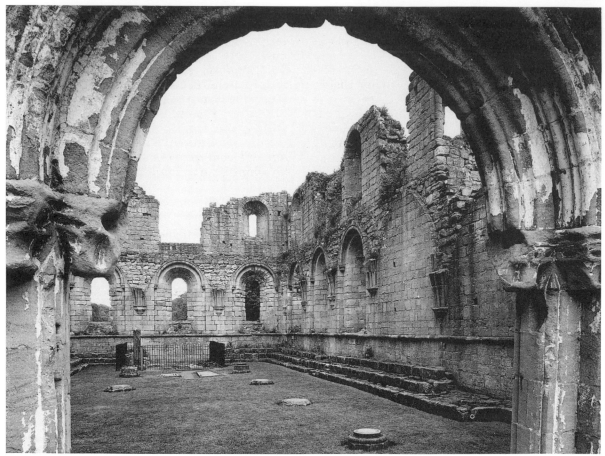

31 *The shattered remains of Richard of Clairvaux's chapter-house retains the bases of its marble piers and the springing and wall ribs of its vaulted ceiling. Within the railings at the east end are the graves of abbots starting with Richard himself and including those of Robert Pipewell, William of Newminster, Ralph Haget, John of York and John of Kent.*

(see **34**). The northern bay was partitioned off to provide a through passage from the cloister to the infirmary. The first two piers from the north are complete, their capitals level with the corbels inserted into the walls of Murdac's range to carry a groin vault. Noticeably, their bases differ from those of the other piers because they are not bases at all but reused capitals which probably came from Murdac's chapter-house. This room remained the day room, still unheated. The day-stair to the dormitory was removed from its northern end, to be replaced by a stair inserted into the east end

of the otherwise untouched south cloister range, a location adopted generally by the order in the third quarter of the twelfth century.

The dormitory itself was almost entirely a new construction, its floor only slightly below the wall-head of Murdac's range. Measuring 54.3m (178ft) long and with a further 17m (55ft) above the projecting part of the chapter-house, it provided sufficient space for 120 monks, their beds placed along the walls and the central part of the room taken up by wooden clothes presses. The main body of the dormitory was lit by alternating tall, round-headed windows and small square lights, while the upper storey of the chapter-house had simply round-headed windows. The raised height of the dormitory floor made the original night-stair to the church unusable, and a new round-headed door was pierced in the south transept gable at the height of the new floor, reached by a timber stair in the transept itself. At the head of the night-stair was a vaulted chamber entered by a wide arch. This was probably the treasury or strong-room in the charge of the sacrist whose bed was placed at the transept end of the dormitory.

The ground floor of the latrine block comprised the novices' day room in many Cistercian houses, and although at Fountains it is now reduced to low walling its original layout is still apparent. It was originally barrel-vaulted and ran the full length of the building. At its east end was an adjoining building that incorporated the east end of the old monks' latrine block and which was aligned north to south, parallel with the dormitory range. This building, much altered in later years, was the abbot's house, its principal rooms at first-floor level with the hall to the north and bed-chamber to the south so that the abbot could maintain a link with the dormitory as he was required to do by the order's statutes. Being built in the late 1160s, it conveniently dates the period at which Cistercian abbots were moving into discrete lodgings.

Enclosed by the east range, the latrine block, the abbot's lodging and the projection of the chapter-house, was a rectangular yard which had a covered alley at least along its west side and perhaps forming, as at Rievaulx, a lesser cloister. Normally, a second cloister was associated with the infirmary where the older members of the community and those who were sick lived a less rigorous life, but at Fountains the early infirmary lies to the north-east of the abbot's house. Only its south wall has been seen in excavation close to its south-west corner, and the line of its west and north walls can be traced from settlement cracks in buildings that now lie over them. Its date of building is unknown, but as it was taken down to extend the church in the second quarter of the thirteenth century it is likely to date either from Richard of Clairvaux's time or immediately afterwards. In plan it is likely to resemble the infirmary built at Rievaulx by Abbot Aelred with a single aisle on its east side. In scale it is much smaller, almost the same size as the early infirmary at Kirkstall. As architectural ideas seem to have been developed within the family of monasteries, it is not surprising that there should be two similar early infirmaries within the Fountains filiation.

The earliest statutes of the order required provision to be made within Cistercian monasteries for hospitality for guests, and Abbot Richard built two guest-houses in the Inner court for the more important visitors to the monastery (32). Each building contained a separate suite of rooms on each floor: a hall with a wall-fireplace, a bed-chamber and a latrine which discharged into the river. The ground-floor suites were vaulted and of inferior quality to those on the upper floors, while the western guest-house was somewhat smaller than its eastern counterpart. Thus accommodation of four different qualities was provided by the two buildings from the 1160s.

The 'sumptuous buildings' of Abbot Robert of Pipewell

Abbot Robert, previously the abbot of Pipewell, was elected in 1170, the first of a series of extremely competent abbots who had trained within the Fountains family. To him fell the completion of the rebuilding of the cloister ranges and church. Serlo records that he was a capable administrator who ruled well and who left behind a name for hospitality to rich and poor alike and who provided his community with 'sumptuous buildings'.

Abbot Pipewell's first work appears to have been the completion of the nave of the church to its original plan and apart from Serlo's statement to that effect there is no other evidence to suggest it had not been completed before his election. However, he also appears to have done some work to the crossing tower, for architectural detail which can only have come from the wall galleries of the lantern has been identified, showing that it was heavily influenced by the crossing towers of Byland Abbey and Ripon Minster, both of which were built early in Robert's abbacy.

He next turned his attention to the completion of the lay brothers' accommodation. The new work can be identified by the use of gothic lancet windows to light the lay brothers' refectory on the ground floor though the windows of the dormitory above continued the original design (33), so far as it could be seen from the Inner Court. It was at this point that the ground-floor rooms were vaulted (34). Both the walls and vault retain extensive traces of the 1170s paint-scheme, a formal masonry pattern similar to that used previously but with the joints picked out by double white lines over a ground coat of limewash. The dormitory on the upper floor was larger than that provided for the lay brothers at Clairvaux itself. On the

32 (Above) The east and west guest-houses built in the 1160s for important visitors to the abbey remain largely as they were first built and are among the best surviving examples of twelfth-century domestic architecture in England. To their east is the gable wall of Abbot Pipewell's lay brothers' infirmary.

33 (Below) Although it was completed over two decades, the west range of the rebuilt stone monastery is remarkable for its general uniformity of style. The ground floor of the earlier, northern end would have been hidden behind high walls that enclosed the cellarer's yards to the west, and it would not have been obvious to medieval visitors that its small round-headed windows differed from the lancet windows that lit the lay brothers' refectory to the south.

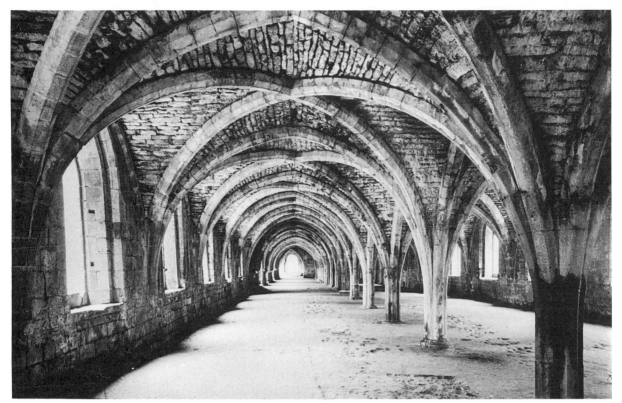

34 *The interior of the west range is now an open space throughout its length but it was originally divided into a series of discrete spaces by cross-walls. Much of the existing vault is twelfth century, though the southernmost bays were reconstructed after they collapsed in the early nineteenth century.*

ground floor, the northern two bays comprised the outer parlour, the next six were cellarage, two bays formed the entry to the cloister and the remaining 12 bays the lay brothers' refectory, following the same general plan as Murdac's original range. Once the west range was finished, the lay brothers' quarters were completed by the building of an infirmary to the west of their latrine block, carried across the river on four tall tunnels. Little now remains other than the north wall (see **32**). It was an aisled hall of six bays, a development in the Early English style that was to become the hallmark of Abbot Pipewell's buildings.

Although Pipewell's work in the west range was impressive it was overshadowed by his achievement in the reconstruction of the south cloister range. With the rebuilding of Clairvaux in the early 1140s, the Benedictine planning of a refectory parallel to the south cloister alley was abandoned and the Cistercians chose to build refectories at right angles to the cloister, allowing the kitchen to occupy the western third of the range where it was accessible from the cloister. By the 1170s, the refectory at Fountains was distinctly old fashioned and the daughter-house of Kirkstall had already built its refectory on a north–south alignment as early as the 1160s and it can only have been the pressure of building elsewhere that resulted in the mother-house taking a further decade to replace its unfashionable refectory.

Abbot Robert's new buildings were purely gothic in style and demonstrate a development of his work in the west range. Here he was building for choir-monks, and the refectory itself was second only in importance to the church and chapter-house. Cistercian conservatism required the suppression of unnecessary ornament but the lightness of the Early English architecture enabled Pipewell to raise buildings that remain beautiful in their simplicity (**35**).

Rebuilding of the south range was a complicated business because it had to be done around

35 *Seen from the lay brothers' dormitory, the composition of Robert of Pipewell's south cloister range is both simple and dramatic in its architecture.*

Murdac's building which remained in use for as long as possible. The earliest part of the new range was the warming-house at its east end, three storeys high. The provision of a warming-house with two great fireplaces 4.9m (16ft) wide marked a softening of the community's austerity, and for the first time there was a heated room accessible from the cloister where fires were burned from 1 November to Good Friday. The fires needed a copious supply of timber to feed them, and a yard was provided to the south of the warming-house that contained a wood-store built against the west wall of the east range. A bridge across the Skell enabled wood to be brought into the yard from the Outer Court of the monastery to the south.

Above the warming-house and reached from the monks' day-stair which occupied the eastern bay of the range, was a dry and fire-proof room, the muniment room in which all the abbey's deeds and estate papers were kept. Its size is not surprising for Fountains had more than 3500 title deeds to its extensive estates, and like many other religious houses safeguarded the deeds and treasure of local families. It was probably here that King John's treasury was kept in the early part of 1215, for nine days after the signing of the *Magna Carta* he ordered that all his goods and valuables stored at Fountains be sent secretly to him. The room was certainly secure, for not only did it have windows with iron grilles and a door closed with a draw-bar set into the masonry, but there were also two further doors in the short passage that led into the room from the day-stair. Further security was ensured by placing the prior's chamber at the head of the day-stair and above the wood-store where he could control access to both the dormitory and the muniment room. Above the muniment room and occupying the roof-space was a further chamber, most probably used for storage but also secure, being reached by a spiral stair from the muniment room passage. The form of its roof, the only roof at Fountains for which there is clear evidence of form, can be reconstructed from the slots and sockets cut into the one surviving warming-house chimney (**36** A and B).

A

B

Muniment room

Daystair

Door to warming house

Lavatorium

Warming house

36 *A reconstruction of the roof above the warming-house and muniment room based on the evidence of slots and sockets in the warming-house chimney.*

Next to be built was the refectory, a remarkable building at the centre of the new south range, its door to the cloister alley flanked by deep arcades that contained the long metal basins of the laver where the monks washed before meals. The pewter troughs of the *lavatorium*, removed at the suppression, were supplied with piped water and the chases for the pipes can still be identified. Indeed, one of the bronze taps (**37**) has survived, recovered by excavation in the nineteenth century. Piped water was generally being introduced into monasteries in the last quarter of the twelfth century, and the Cistercians were in the vanguard of this development. At Fountains, two supplies were required, one for the choir-monks and a second for the lay brothers. Water was collected on the south side of the precinct (see

Chapter 5) and piped to the cloister buildings through a series of well-houses (of which the late twelfth-century 'Robin Hood's well' is the only survivor) and conduits. Little is known of the water supply at Fountains because it has yet to be examined by excavation, but examination of the contemporary waterworks at Kirkstall has shown that it is likely to be very sophisticated.

The refectory was conceived as a building of five double bays with a central arcade, each bay lit by a pair of tall lancet windows. Its length posed a problem because the old yard to the south of Murdac's refectory in which it was built was bounded to the south again by the river, leaving insufficient space for the new building. The river could not be moved for it flushed both the lay brothers' and monks' latrines, and the only solution was to build the southernmost half-bay of the building over the river on a tunnel. Construction was from south to north, with a temporary pause against the south wall of the earlier refectory which

51

37 *A cast bronze tap from the cloister laver gives a clue to the decoration that the Cistercians had come to accept by the last quarter of the twelfth century. Its survival in use up to the sixteenth century shows how reliable the piped water system at Fountains was.*

38 *The refectory has lost the arcade down its centre which supported its double-pitched roof, and the reader's pulpit has gone, but it still retains the foot-paces around its walls and the stone legs of its tables. The twelfth-century roof was replaced by one of flat pitch in the late fifteenth century but the gable wall still retains the bottoms of two circular windows that filled its original double gable.*

remained in use as long as possible. Finally, a section of the old refectory was demolished and the rebuilding completed (**38**), the new work being carried out in stone of a slightly different colour leaving a joint which is still apparent.

Within, the new refectory was an impressive building, open to the roof and divided down its centre by an arcade. As originally built, the refectory was roofed in two spans, a feature of the contemporary refectory at Fontenay, and each span was lit by a circular window in its southern gable. The roof was altered to one of a single span and lower pitch in the fifteenth century but otherwise the refectory retains its original detailing. The walls were whitewashed and lined out in white paint to resemble ashlar masonry, and although most of this has now been lost, some remains in the splays of the western windows, showing that the monotony of plain block-work was relieved with geometric patterns which perhaps reflected the *grisaille* windows (**colour plate 7**).

Raised footpaces or platforms were provided against the east and west walls and these retain the bases of the stone legs that supported long tables for the monks, whose benches were placed against the side walls, three on the east and only two on the west as access to the kitchen precluded a third table. The tunnel that carried the southern half-bay of the building over the Skell provided the base for a broad dais on which the prior's table was set. Because custom required the abbot to eat with guests, the prior was to preside over the convent's meals, twice a day in summer and once in winter. Meals were taken in silence, only interrupted by readings from the Bible. A round-headed door in the west wall led to a stair in the thickness of the wall that gave access to a passage and the reader's pulpit carried on a great foliate corbel that still remains.

The last part of the south range to be rebuilt was the kitchen, placed to serve both the monks' refectory and that of the lay brothers in the west range. A round-headed opening to the monks' refectory was not a door for the jambs are convex, instead the opening was originally fitted with a circular dumb-waiter revolving on a pivot. A similar, smaller opening to the lay brothers' refectory once existed but has been blocked up. At the centre of the kitchen, which prepared only vegetarian dishes as meat was not allowed to healthy monks, were two great fireplaces set back-to-back with a chimney passing up through the roof. As originally built

the kitchen was open to the roof. To reduce the heat, three unglazed pointed arches pierced the north wall above the cloister roof and a wide archway was provided in the south wall. This door led to a yard on the south side of the kitchen where wood to feed the fires was stored. Kitchens were a notorious fire-risk, and shortly after the completion of Abbot Robert's new kitchen vaulted ceilings were inserted to the north and south of the chimney stack to protect the roof. Though they no longer survive, clear traces can be seen of three bays of vaulting in the northern half of the building, and two to the south of the chimney.

39 *Reconstructed from fragments dumped in the east guest-house in the late eighteenth century, Robert of Pipewell's cloister arcade is the most elaborate of the twelfth-century Cistercian cloister arcades known in England. The leaf decoration of its marble capitals has been omitted in this drawing.*

40ft

60   60

0

40 *On the death of Abbot Pipewell, the rebuilt
stone monastery was complete, its buildings
comparing well with any other great Cistercian
house in Europe, and providing a convincing
illustration of the scale and disposition of the
central buildings of the head of a family.*

The final work which can be attributed to
Robert of Pipewell was the construction of a
splendid new cloister arcade (**39**), linking the
newly complete cloister ranges and church and
providing the monks' living room at the heart
of the monastery. Though ruthlessly swept
away in the 1770s, many of its elements have
been discovered and it is possible to reconstruct
it with a high degree of accuracy. Twin shafts of
black Nidderdale 'marble' with matching capitals and bases supported pointed trefoil arches
of sandstone which were white-limed to provide
contrast. Porches projected into the cloister
garth at the centre of the north and south
alleys. That on the north contained the abbot's
seat where he heard Collation, that to the
south had a door that matched that of the

refectory and provided the entrance to the
cloister garth itself where there was probably a
garden. Although the openings were not
glazed, the cloister alleys at Fountains were
the finest constructed by the Cistercians in
England, and if they lacked the simplicity that
St Bernard sought, they amply demonstrated
the importance of the abbey as the mother
house of an important family.

The death of Abbot Robert in 1180 marks the
completion of the second major stage in the
history of the abbey (**40**). The community had
been provided with a great church and fine
cloister buildings that reflected the house's
importance within the order, it had expanded
to its optimum size, and it had achieved sufficient wealth to support itself and to indulge in
monumental building works. Now was the time
for a period of consolidation, with abbots more
noted for their spirituality than their administrative genius. The purpose of the community
was after all to praise God through prayer,
meditation and manual labour, and great
building works must have been a dreadful
distraction.

4

The softening of Cistercian ideals

The election of William of Newminster as abbot in 1180 marked the start of a period of consolidation. An old man wasted by continual austerity, he had been professed at Augustinian Gisborough but had joined the Cistercians at Newminster and in time became the abbot there. He was not a builder, but a wise and vigorous administrator who ruled with gentleness. Dying in 1190, he was succeeded by Ralph Haget, an ex-soldier who had entered Fountains on the advice of his friend Sinnulph, a lay brother of the house. For nine years he had been abbot of the daughter-house of Kirkstall where he had proved to be of no great administrative ability. His greatest qualities were his spirituality, wit and charm. In him the community found a leader they could love and respect. He died in 1203, and his death marks the beginning of the next phase in the abbey's development. It also marked a change in the order, for from the beginning of the thirteenth century, the Cistercians began to lose many of the characteristics that had set them apart from unreformed Benedictines. In particular, this softening of ideals is demonstrated in the new buildings raised at Fountains during the first half of the thirteenth century.

The rebuilding of the abbey church

By 1180, after less than half a century, the buildings of Fountains Abbey had achieved a greater scale than any other house of the order in England, including the great neighbouring abbey of Rievaulx. Between 1203 and 1247 the abbey was to see even more extensive building, as the Cistercians became wealthier and willing to accept a lessening degree of architectural puritanism. Richard of Clairvaux's choir and presbytery of the 1150s was no longer fashionable and the convent found their church cramped and dark. It was decided to replace the old two-bay presbytery with a great aisled eastern arm of five bays. The building of this occupied the abbacies of three Johns: John of York, John of Hessle and John of Kent.

John of York, who became abbot on Haget's death, had a similar career to his predecessor. In turn he had been a monk, then cellarer of Fountains, and then abbot of the colony of Louth Park before he returned to the mother house. To him belongs the decision to rebuild the eastern part of the church. The model he chose to follow was the four-bay aisled choir-arm of Jervaulx Abbey which had only recently been completed. Jervaulx appears to have been the first church in England where the Cistercians had adopted a form of aisled choir-arm with a stark, square east wall already used by both the Benedictines at Whitby and Tynemouth, and the Augustinians at Hexham. Although the church of Jervaulx has been destroyed to the level of its plinth, large numbers of its architectural elements can still be identified on site and the technical similarities that these pieces display to the surviving structure at Fountains would suggest that the same master mason was involved. The height of the existing transepts and nave required that the new work should match the two-storey elevation of Richard of Clairvaux's church, but in architectural terms it was a very different building. Gone were the heavy cylindrical piers of the nave, round-headed windows, and boarded wooden roof of the main span. In their place was a light and very gothic structure with tall lancet windows, a wealth of moulded detail and a vaulted ceiling over the main span as well as the aisles. Only the outer walls of this

new presbytery survive, for the arcades had fallen and been cleared away by the third quarter of the eighteenth century (**colour plate 8**). Enough remains, however to reconstruct its elevations with a high degree of accuracy (**41**).

The new aisles opened out of the inner mid-twelfth-century transept chapels, and were divided from the main body of the presbytery by alternating piers of octagonal and clustered form. Along the outer walls was an arcade with trefoiled heads supported on detached shafts of Nidderdale 'marble'. The arcade was set above a wall-bench and mirrored a freestanding arcade within the main vessel that enclosed the high altar and the area before it. The aisles were lit by lancet windows with *grisaille* glass in wooden frames, for which the fixings can still be seen, flanked by rather curious arcading that follows the profile of the vault. Fallen detail from the upper part of the presbytery shows that its clerestory matched that of later work further to the east. The traditional upper storeys of triforium and clerestory were combined, with a single lancet window flanked by blind arcades fronted by a wall-passage and gallery framed by the wall-ribs of the high vault. The walls were covered with a buff limewash on which false ashlar jointing was painted to contrast with the framing of the black Nidderdale 'marble' shafts used throughout the building.

John of York must have begun this project towards the end of his abbacy, for at his death in 1211, the *Narratio* records that he had only completed a few of the piers. Presumably he was building around the earlier church and the old presbytery would only be demolished when the new choir arm was reaching completion. His successor, John of Hessle, who left Fountains in 1220 to become Bishop of Ely, must have completed the work and brought the new building of five bays into the church. In spite of the monks' complaint that their choir in the crossing and eastern bay of the nave was cramped and dark, it remained there until the

suppression of the monasteries. Rievaulx was quick to follow Fountains' lead, beginning the construction of an aisled choir-arm of seven bays in the second decade of the thirteenth century that was conceived from the first as a much grander and more expensive building of three full storeys. It brought Rievaulx close to bankruptcy and caused Fountains to think bigger.

The buildings of Abbot John of Kent

John of Kent's greatest contribution was the addition of an eastern transept, the Chapel of Nine Altars, to the east of the new presbytery. This remarkable building remains virtually intact apart from its roof and vaults. It has no Cistercian model (**42**), indeed the only comparable building is the eastern transept of the Benedictine cathedral-priory of Durham begun

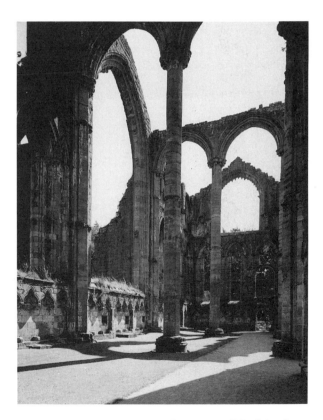

41 *Reconstructed from surviving fallen elements, three bays of the early thirteenth-century presbytery show that it was a sophisticated composition which contrasted strongly with the stark simplicity of the earlier nave and transepts (Stuart Harrison).*

42 *The Chapel of Nine Altars, modified in the late fifteenth century when its vaults were removed and new windows inserted, continues the architectural design of the presbytery to which it was added in the second quarter of the thirteenth century.*

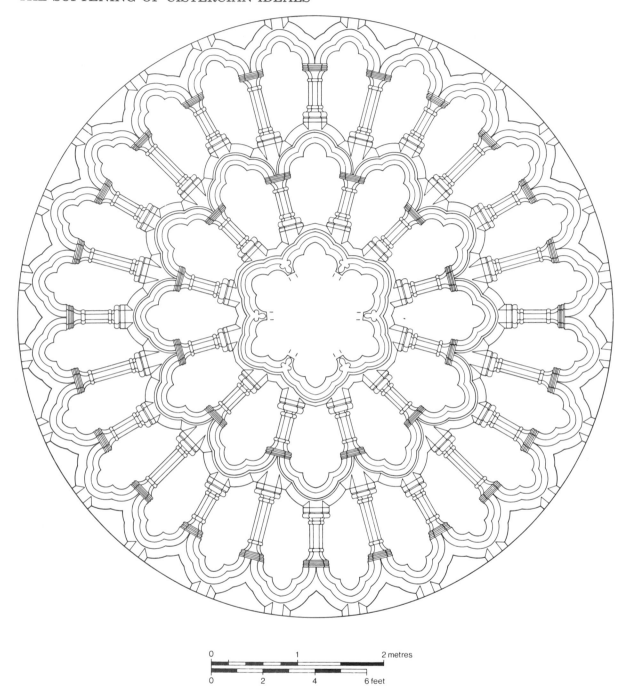

0   1   2 metres

0   2   4   6 feet

43 *The rose window from the eastern gable of the church comprised three rings of trefoiled lights. No parts of the outer ring have yet been recovered but its form is presumed to replicate the other lights of the window* (Stuart Harrison).

in 1242 as a copy of the Fountains building. It effectively added two bays to the length of the presbytery and was nine bays in length. It was built to provide a series of nine chapels against the east wall of the church, needed by the growing number of monks who were also priests and required to say a personal Mass. The fact that Clairvaux had nine chapels around its eastern apse is significant, for Fountains, rather than Rievaulx which had the better claim, was projecting itself as the 'English Clairvaux'.

Architecturally, the Chapel of Nine Altars continued the design of the presbytery, though its detailing shows a degree of development. Each bay had a lancet window flanked by blind arcading set over a continuous wall arcade that matched those of the presbytery aisles, with a similar arrangement in the clerestory fronted by a wall passage and gallery. In the eastern gable of the church, in place of the three central lancets of the clerestory, was a great rose window, removed in 1483 by Abbot Darnton, that balanced Richard of Clairvaux's circular window in the west gable of the nave. Many elements from this window have been recovered (43) showing that it was an elaborate feature, a contrasting combination of black Nidderdale 'marble' shafts and white-painted gritstone rings set within a heavily moulded rim, picked out with red and black paint. The inner face of the rose window was rebated to take glazed panels set in wooden frames which must have been fixed in position as the window was constructed and acted as centring. The design of the rose window was reflected in the multicoloured mosaic tile floor that was then laid in the presbytery and Nine Altars, fragments of which can still be seen reset in the platform of the high altar. Sadly, no major areas of Abbot John's pavements laid after 1236 have survived in place. This is particularly unfortunate for they are likely to have been the first use of mosaic tiles by the Cistercians in northern England. Only the Cistercian abbey of Beaulieu in Hampshire has produced earlier tiles, dated to the completion of the presbytery there in about 1227. The form of the Fountains pavements must have been similar to those that still survive at Byland (**colour plate 9**).

Although the inspiration for the new presbytery was entirely English, indeed the same master was responsible for the eastern arm of Beverley Minster where identical detailing can still be seen, there remained a strong element of Cistercian restraint apparent in the architecture. Dog-tooth decoration, much loved by both Benedictines and Augustinians, was noticeably absent, only occurring on the rim of the eastern rose window, and the keystones of the high vaults and aisle vaults were not decorated with carved bosses but were simply distinguished by being cut from Nidderdale 'marble' to contrast with the gritstone used for the web of ribs. Although more elaborate than the mid-twelfth-century scheme that survived in the nave and transepts, there was a studied formality to the decoration of the presbytery and Nine Altars that was peculiarly Cistercian.

John of Kent's extension of the presbytery to build the Nine Altars was achievable only at a cost. While most of the new building lay in the convent cemetery, the south-eastern corner of the new transept required the demolition of the infirmary that occupied that part of the site. As a consequence, he was also obliged to build a new infirmary and one that was to accord with the size and status of his monastery. It had to lie to the south of the church so that it was accessible from the cloister but there was insufficient space to the north of the river on which to build, and the land rose too steeply on the south bank of the Skell, preventing building there. Four great tunnels some 75m (245ft) long were constructed across the river in a remarkable feat of engineering to provide a platform on which the new infirmary could be built (44). Little remains of the new infirmary except low walling and foundations, but its excavation in the mid-nineteenth century recovered many fragments of its superstructure.

This infirmary was one of the largest aisled halls ever built in medieval England. It comprised a hall of eight bays, flanked by aisles which were carried around the ends of the building. Fireplaces were situated centrally in its north and south walls, and beds were ranged along the side walls. Each bay of the side walls had a single window of two lights with a circular light in the plate tracery of the head, rebated for shutters or more probably to hold glass in wooden frames (45). The arcades were supported by elegant circular piers with bandings and four detached shafts of Nidderdale 'marble'. The fallen springers of the arcade that remain, plain towards the aisles but finely

44 *John of Kent's new infirmary was built on tunnels over the river, and though it is now ruined to the level of its plinths, enough detail survives to reconstruct its original form, one of the largest aisled halls ever built in medieval England.*

moulded towards the nave, indicate that the aisles were not vaulted but had open timber roofs. The nave had no clerestory but the whole building was covered with a single roof. Perhaps more than any other building at Fountains, this grand new infirmary, itself a separate monastery for the old and infirm members of the community, indicates the wealth and status that Fountains Abbey had achieved by the second quarter of the thirteenth century.

Abbot John also provided other buildings within the infirmary complex, for his tunnels provided a platform for building to the east and west of the infirmary hall. Only one of these has survived later rebuilding, a two-storey block to the east of the hall and separated from it by a small yard. Its original use is not certain. To the west of the infirmary and above the two

45 *Two of the window-heads recovered from the infirmary by excavation in the 1850s and which give a good impression of the quality of the building (Simon Hayfield).*

0   ·5   1 metre

0   1   2   3 feet

46 *Many architectural elements survive from John of Kent's cloister arcade which have enabled its accurate reconstruction (*Stuart Harrison*).*

northern tunnels is a much altered building which in its original form was the infirmary latrine block. Seven latrine shafts on the line of the south wall discharge into the river below, and as they are contemporary with the construction of the tunnels themselves this building must be a part of John of Kent's original building.

Connecting the infirmary to the cloister ranges and church was a gallery (**46**), which can be identified with John of Kent's new cloister, its walls pierced with open arcades. The eastern half of the gallery with a passage to the north connecting with the south end of the Chapel of the Nine Altars was built first, lit by groups of three trefoil-headed unglazed openings supported on twin shafts in both walls. Between the openings were short lengths of walling with blind arcading, strengthened by shallow external buttresses. John of Kent's infirmary cloister must have been an exquisite structure. Either John, or perhaps less likely his successor Stephen of Eston, completed the gallery to the west, where the architectural detailing was slightly more developed.

Apart from two remarkable buildings in the

47 *The enclosing precinct wall stands to full height on both the west and south sides of the abbey.*

Outer Court very little remains of Abbot John's other buildings. His recorded work in the guest-house complex is largely unknown but must have been substantial. Of his almonry, nothing at all is known, not even its site, though it must lie on the west side of the Inner Court to the west of the guest-houses. One further major structure, the precinct wall (**47**), appears to date from John's abbacy though it might have been begun during that of John of Hessle, for it contains reused architectural detail that can only have come from the east end of the mid-twelfth-century church. This wall, 3.4m (12ft) high to the top of its coping, enclosed the abbey on the west, south, and east sides, defining a precinct of some 28.3 ha (70 acres). The north side was closed by the quarried cliff face that still defines the north side of the Skell valley. Somewhat smaller than the 37.2 ha (92 acres) of the enclosed precinct at Rievaulx, it was still a substantial area to enclose. The average extent of a monastic precinct in England was roughly 10 ha (25 acres).

On John's death in 1247, Fountains had experienced four major building campaigns in 115 years, and the community must have longed for a succession of abbots who did not wish to make their mark as builders. In this they were fortunate, for on the completion of John's schemes, the abbey was to see no major building work until the second half of the fifteenth century. In any case, the buildings of Fountains Abbey in 1250 would have stood a favourable comparison with any other major monastery in Europe (**48**).

Fountains in the thirteenth and fourteenth centuries

On John of Kent's death, Fountains was at the height of its wealth and prestige. Twelfth-century land grants and sound estate management, coupled with the exploitation of an army of lay brothers, had made the abbey the richest of its order in England. Much of the wealth was derived from sheep, though the abbey had developed a mixed economy. Although the annual wool-clip provided sufficient to meet the running costs of the house and had funded the building work of the late twelfth and early thirteenth centuries it was subject to the vagaries of the market-place. Wool brought ready money, it could also bring disaster. It was sold to the great continental firms of wool-merchants, sometimes several years in advance against a substantial payment, providing a ready temptation for the convent to anticipate its real revenue. If the clip fell short of the contract, the house was obliged to make up the deficit. This happened to Fountains in the second half of the thirteenth century, bringing the house to the verge of bankruptcy. By 1274, the abbey was £900 in debt to the Jews of York because of wool speculation, and although the king installed a lay commissioner, Peter Willoughby, to sort out the abbey's finances, renewed speculation by Abbots Peter Ayling (who pledged the abbey itself as security for a four-year contract to supply wool to Florentine merchants), Henry Otley and Robert Thornton left the abbey in debt to the tune of £6373 by 1291. Then the king was forced to impose his justiciar John of Berwick on the convent to achieve some measure of financial stability. The founding community would have been appalled, not only by such

40ft
60   60
0

48 *The central buildings of the abbey had reached their greatest extent by 1250 when Fountains was at the height of its power and influence and were to remain in this form until the last decades of the fifteenth century.*

dreadful mismanagement but also by the willingness of the community to involve itself with money. Gone was the poverty and simplicity of life.

For all its problems, the abbey was still a major power in the land. It settled down to a period of relative stability, reflected more in its buildings than in the spirituality of its monks. Throughout the late thirteenth and fourteenth centuries, no major buildings were raised and any work that was undertaken was in the area of the infirmary, the abbot's house, the guest-houses and the buildings of the Outer Court, largely indicative of the changes in monastic life and economy seen elsewhere at this period.

The alteration of the church to suit a changing way of life

The period 1265 to 1436 was one of crisis and controversy for Fountains, with domestic mismanagement and national crisis overshadowing religious life. For ten years after the defeat of the English army at Bannockburn in 1314, the north was destabilized by Scottish raids, and the abbey itself was occupied by a large part of the Scots army in 1318. Abbot Walter Coxwold, hard pressed to maintain his convent,

was required to raise men for the king to fight the Scots in 1318 and 1321, and in 1322 against the abortive rebellion of the Earl of Lancaster. The spirit of lawlessness pervading the north continued until the middle years of the fourteenth century and had a drastic effect on the economic and religious life of the abbey. With many of its estates bordering on ruin, Fountains could no longer rely on a steady supply of recruits for its army of lay brothers and by the middle of the fourteenth century they had virtually ceased to exist as a separate class within the monastery. Indeed, in 1380/81 only 34 monks and 10 lay brothers are recorded in the abbey.

The ruined shell of the abbey church shows little indication that it had been altered since the completion of the Chapel of Nine Altars, so thoroughly has it been stripped of its fittings. However, major changes did take place from the early fourteenth century which can be reconstructed from the little evidence that does survive. The removal of the lay brothers' choir from the nave permitted a major replanning of the church, displaying a development of the Cistercian liturgy (**49**). Precisely when this happened is uncertain but the new layout pre-dated the burial of Abbot John Ripon in 1434/5. We know that Fountains' daughter-house of Meaux underwent a similar replanning in the 1390s and it is unlikely that the mother-house would not have reorganized its church before then.

63

49 *The later medieval planning of the church can be determined from the marks left by its screens on the masonry and by the evidence of excavation and documents. This plan shows features from the fourteenth to sixteenth centuries and should be compared with* **27**. *1–6 are identified graves of abbots, 7 that of a late cellarer of the house and 8 that of a major patron.*

A reduced income seems to have resulted in a reduced number of choir-monks, for the monks' choir was reduced in length by a bay from the west and a new pulpitum screen provided between the first pair of piers west of the crossing. The bay of the nave thus emptied was provided with a great loft at the height of the old pulpitum screen that remained between the second pair of piers. On this loft, which extended into the north aisle, was an organ, for which the fixings of the case remain in the spandrels of the north arcade. Meaux had two organs in 1396, 'the great organ at the west end of the nave and a lesser organ in the choir' and it is quite possible that the same provision was made at Fountains in the later fourteenth century. Below the loft, parclose screens were placed between the nave piers, to enclose the lower entry to the choir. West of the old pulpitum, the chapels of St Mary and St Bernard were retained and the retrochoir in the fourth bay was provided with benches between the piers of the arcades. Because the aisles no longer functioned as through-passages, they could be partitioned off to provide individual chapels, five in the south aisle and four in the north, their altars set against the west face of the arcade piers where the tiled platforms of three can still be seen. Such chapels are a common feature of Cistercian churches and can still be seen at Byland and Roche, and were provided at Rievaulx from the later years of the thirteenth century. Little trace now remains of these chapels at Fountains, for their timber parclose screens have left only the evidence of their fixings in the masonry. At Rievaulx, a list of their furnishings has survived, showing that their altars were substantially dressed, and it is possible that four fragments derived from two altar retables depicting the four Evangelists (**50**) were a part of the furnishings of these new side chapels.

A second major change was the permitting of burials within the church, first of major patrons and later of abbots. Patronal burials had long been allowed in the cemetery and the cloister, and a group of such burials is known outside the chapter-house. The northernmost burial of

50 *Part of a fourteenth-century retable, one of two by the same carver found at Fountains, depicting St Luke, author of the third Gospel, shown seated with a pen and scroll. It probably comes from one of the nave chapels but its findspot is not recorded.*

this group, which lay outside the entrance to the library, was found on excavation to date to the later twelfth century. This group of burials is likely to include William de Percy II who died in about 1174. By the early thirteenth century, burials were being placed in the galilee porch at the west end of the church, two perhaps being the burials of William de Stuteville and Matilda Countess of Warwick who both died in 1203. The convent must have been coming under increasing pressure to permit burials within the church itself as other orders allowed. At Bordesley Abbey, the only Cistercian house to have provided detailed information, excavation has shown that burial in the church began in the late thirteenth century. Judging from surviving effigies at Cistercian houses such as Furness, Abbey Dore, Deer, Dundrennan, Hailes, Rievaulx, Jervaulx, Kirkstead, Margam, Neath and Strata Florida, patronal burial within the church began in the last quarter of the thirteenth century.

The first recorded burial in the presbytery at Fountains was of Roger, Lord Mowbray, in 1298. The site of his burial is not known but a coffin between the second and third piers of the north arcade marks a patronal burial and others probably occupy the spaces between the other piers, lining the open space before the high altar, their superstructures replacing the trefoil-headed arcade that had enclosed the altar space. What had been reserved as a liturgical area was now given over as a mausoleum for the great northern families whose ancestors had endowed the abbey. In 1315, Henry Percy, Lord of Alnwick, was buried in the centre of the presbytery before the high altar itself, and his tomb-cover has survived, a military figure in a voluminous hauberk of chain-mail (**51**). Fountains was no longer just the workplace of the *new soldiers of Christ*, it was now the burial place of the old military order.

Where the laity began, abbots were soon to follow. As the chapter-house filled up, they turned their eyes to the church. The first abbot to be buried there, behind the high altar at the centre of the Nine Altars, was William Gower who died in 1384. The next president-burial was that of Robert Burley in 1410 at the centre of the choir. A fragment of his Nidderdale 'marble' tomb-slab now lies in the northern chapel of the south transept. He was followed in 1435 by Abbot John Ripon whose grave was

51 *The tomb-effigy of Henry Percy of Alnwick, showing a knight wearing a voluminous hauberk of chain mail beneath a sleeveless surcoat, is a product of the Cheyne workshop in York. Traces of paint survive. It originally covered his tomb that lay in the centre of the presbytery before the high altar, though it has moved about the site since the suppression. It was broken by drunken militia-men in about 1800 (*Simon Hayfield*).*

placed in the retrochoir. The next abbot, John Martin, was buried to the east of Ripon in 1442, and his successor Thomas Paslew was buried the following year at the entrance to the choir. Finally, Thomas Swinton was buried after 1478 between the monks' choir and the presbytery step, his gravestone with the indent of a now-missing brass (**52**) still visible in the turf.

52 *The ledger slab of Abbot Thomas Swinton's grave survives between the eastern crossing piers. Although the brass insets have been plundered and the stone broken by Walbran's labourers when it was discovered in 1840, the outline of the abbot's figure with a mitre above his head and below a canopy can still be observed. The placing of the mitre is a reference to Swinton's resignation in 1478 (Simon Hayfield).*

Further modification of the church in the late fifteenth and early sixteenth centuries

By the second half of the fifteenth century, the structure of the church was beginning to show its age and there is evidence to suggest that both the crossing and the eastern arm were failing structurally. Abbot Greenwell had improved the interior of the church, laying new tile pavements in the transepts and nave, and provided a stone night-stair from the church to the dormitory, but he did nothing to repair or modernize the building itself. It fell to two of the greatest abbots of the house, John Darnton and Marmaduke Huby, to restore the church to a state fitting for the greatest and richest house of the Cistercian order in England.

Abbot Darnton inherited a church that was distinctly old-fashioned and showing signs of instability. Stresses from the crossing tower and the presbytery had caused the south-eastern crossing pier to deform and a huge buttress had been built to support it. Poor maintenance and over-ambitious building was starting to take its toll. Darnton found that the high vaults of the presbytery and Chapel of Nine Altars were in a dangerous state. The south-east corner of the Nine Altars was so unstable as to require shoring up. His reaction was to remodel the eastern part of the church, removing the vaults of the main vessels, cutting back their springers, and replacing them with a new timber roof (**colour plate 10**). Where the masonry had faulted over windows he inserted stitches of new stone. A gap in the head of the north window of the east wall of the Nine Altars was patched with a stone carved with the head of a 'green man' and an angel carrying a scroll with the date 1483, while the head of the east window of the south wall was repaired with a figure of St James of Compostella supported on the head of an abbot, perhaps a portrait of Darnton himself (**53**). He went on to modernize the Chapel of Nine Altars with the insertion of new windows in the north and south gables, and a vast east window of nine lights that occupied the three central bays of the chapel and removed all the original fenestration and intervening wall there. Externally, great buttresses were built to support the central part of the Nine Altars. Below the great new window, the three central chapels were united as a single chapel. Examination of the thirteenth-century windows of the presbytery and Nine Altars shows that the original glazing in wooden frames was removed at this time and replaced by new glass set into the masonry. Only fragments of the borders now survive but loose fragments of glass show that the new glazing was pictorial rather than geometric.

Once the repair of the eastern arm was complete, John Darnton turned his attention to the transepts and nave which he re-roofed at the lower pitch he had established for the presbytery. The reduction in pitch suggests that it was only then that the roofs were covered with lead, and a reduction in the pitch of the refectory roof would suggest that this improvement was not simply restricted to the church.

The twelfth-century nave was distinctly old-fashioned but little used except for the chapels in the aisles. However, Darnton replaced all but two of the aisle windows with more modern traceried lights (**54**). The windows he left unaltered were those that lit the choir entrance below the loft of the pulpitum and which were barely visible inside the building. He also provided a new west window to balance the east window of the presbytery, completing the work in the year before his death. Above the window in the west wall of the church is a niche containing a statue of the Virgin and Child supported on a bracket carved with an eagle (associated with St John) and a barrel or tun with the letters DERN and the date 1494 on a scroll. This carving, or *rebus*, puns on the name John Darnton and is effectively his signature on the completion of his work. Of Darnton's internal decoration of the church there is little evidence. He redecorated the eastern arm by overpainting the original painted masonry pattern with plain limewash, but he must also have refitted the chapels of the Nine Altars and the nave that he had altered. Perhaps it was from one of those that three alabaster retable panels come (**55**).

53 *A repair by John Darnton of a dislocated window head in the south wall of the Nine Altars was carved with a portrait of Darnton himself wearing a mitre and supporting two dolphins and a scroll (which probably carried his motto 'Benedicite Fontes Domino') below a figure of St James of Compostella, identified by a cockle shell on his purse (Judith Dobie).*

Although Abbot Darnton had modernized the structure of the church, his work is overshadowed by that of his successor, Marmaduke Huby. Abbot Huby was a great builder, made more significant than his predecessor because his principal contribution to the abbey survives. In common with most Cistercian churches, Fountains had no great bell-tower but simply a lantern tower at the crossing which had been causing concern since the late fourteenth century. Huby's first plan seems to have been to build a new crossing tower. His work can be identified by the widespread use of magnesian limestone, first used in Darnton's building, and by the frequent use of his initials and motto. First, the weakness in the eastern crossing piers was corrected and the arch into the south presbytery aisle was underbuilt with a substantial new arch carried on a reinforced timber raft, and then wide cracks in the failing

54 *One of the new windows provided by John Darnton lights an extension to the inner chapel of the south transept that he extended to form a sacristy. Identical windows were inserted in the north and south aisles of the nave.*

55 *Three fifteenth-century alabaster panels from an incomplete retable found at Fountains in the early nineteenth century. They illustrate scenes from the life of the Virgin: on the left the Assumption; in the centre the Coronation of the Virgin; and on the right the Nativity. All bear traces of polychrome decoration.*

57 *Huby's tower was built for show and remains a powerful reminder of the abbey's power and influence.*

56 *Huby's repair of the crossing required the insertion of a new arch into the south aisles of the presbytery and the filling of an alarming crack in the wall above the original arch. This photograph, taken in the early 1930s shows areas of twelfth-century limewash which have now largely disappeared.*

masonry of the east wall of the south transept were repaired (**56**). However, Huby's masons must have thought it better to abandon that scheme and consider a new tower elsewhere.

The late fifteenth century was a period of tower-building in the north of England, and the Cumberland abbeys of Shap and Furness both built monumental western towers to house peals of bells and to mark their status. Abbot Redman of Shap was the Bishop of Ely and Visitor of the English province of Premonstratensian canons, of comparable rank to Huby who was the commissary of the abbot of Cîteaux. Huby chose unusually to build his new

tower at the end of the north transept. The scale and design of this new tower (**57**) amply demonstrated Fountains' importance as the pre-eminent Cistercian house in England and the status of Abbot Huby, that 'golden and unbreakable column in his zeal for the order'.

Huby's tower survives intact but for its floors, roof, bells and some window tracery, 48.7m (160ft) high and of four stages. It was a tower designed to impress, rising from a deep, moulded plinth and supported by massive angle buttresses. Externally it is divided into four storeys by string-courses which correspond approximately to its internal floors, and is topped by an embattled parapet which originally had tall pinnacles at the angles standing on the buttresses and connected to the wall-head by miniature flying buttresses, with small pinnacles corbelled out from the parapet in the middle of each side. The windows of each stage vary: the ground and second floors have standard Perpendicular traceried windows with pointed heads that would have matched closely Abbot Darnton's new windows in the church itself, the first floor has similar windows with elliptical heads, and the fourth floor has three-light windows with square heads. The bell-chamber occupied the third floor and its windows were closed with wooden louvres, otherwise all the windows were glazed.

The proportions of the tower are enhanced by its decoration. The angle buttresses have tall niches under gabled heads which were designed to take statues though none ever appear to have been fixed. Above seven of the windows are smaller niches, five of which retain statues. On the south face above the lowest window is the statue of an abbot without a mitre, perhaps St Bernard, while above the lowest window of the north face is St Catherine and above the second window St James the Great. The statues above the lowest windows on the east and west faces of the tower are angels holding shields, that on the east bearing the three horseshoes of Fountains, that on the west the mitre, staff and initials of Huby himself. Bands of black-letter inscription 0.6m (2ft) high were placed below the parapet and beneath the upper two tiers of windows, comprising Latin texts taken from the Cistercian breviary. The upper bands are badly eroded but still partly legible, the lowest which runs only round the east, north and west faces of the tower reads 'REGI AUTEM SAECULORUM IMMORTALI, INVISIBLI, SOLI DEO, HONORE ET GLORIA IN SAECULA SAECULORUM' ('now unto the King Eternal, Immortal, Invisible, the Only God, be honour and glory for ever'), repeated four times. It was from this verse, taken from St Paul's first epistle to Timothy, that Huby derived his personal motto 'Soli Deo honor et gloria' used on many of his buildings.

Within the church, Huby's hand can be seen in continuing improvements. A new pulpitum screen was provided between the second pair of piers in the nave and new choir-stalls were provided for the thirty or so monks who now occupied the abbey. The stalls are gone, but were probably the work of the Bromflete family of Ripon who were providing new stalls and screenwork for the monks of Jervaulx (**colour plate 11**) and canons of Bridlington and Easby at this time. Their site is marked by stone-lined pits (now reburied), which comprised a hollow space below the wooden floor of the stalls to give more resonance to the singing. This effect was further heightened in the northern bank of stalls by the inclusion of open-necked pottery jars in the stone lining of the pit. In the nave, Huby added statue brackets to the fourth pier from the west of the north arcade and fifth pier of the south arcade, and placed a series of limestone markers in the nave floor that indicated the positions to be taken by members of the community when they visited the nave on their Sunday procession.

The monks' lives outside their church were also changing, and although the main cloister ranges remained unaltered there are indications that they were made more comfortable and less draughty. A smaller number of monks would permit the partitioning of the dormitory to provide more private cells for instance, but Fountains does not display the same degree of growing comfort in its cloister ranges that many monasteries do. Even in the sixteenth century, Abbot William Thirsk was able to claim that the traditions of his 'religion' set apart the behaviour of his order from others. Substantial changes did occur at Fountains but not within the confines of the cloister.

Alterations to the infirmary

The development of monastic life in the late thirteenth and fourteenth centuries can best be seen in the way the infirmary buildings were adapted (**58**). What had begun its life as a monastery within a monastery for the old and sick became a more important element in the lives of the whole community.

In the late thirteenth century, the building to the north-east of the infirmary hall was converted to provide a home for Abbot Peter Ayling who resigned in 1279. At the same time, a new chapel was provided to the south, presumably replacing a smaller chapel provided by John of Kent. Ayling's house communicated by a mural stair with this chapel, enabling him to hear divine service while avoiding the community he had scandalized and almost bankrupted (see p.62). The softer lifestyle of the infirmary was perhaps more to the taste of an ex-abbot than a return to the life of the cloister. Old and sick monks had always been allowed richer food than the rest of the community and this included both meat and eggs, which were proscribed in the refectory. After 1300, the Benedictines relaxed their rule to permit the occasional eating of meat by the community,

58 *In plan, the infirmary shows evidence of being altered throughout the fourteenth, fifteenth and sixteenth centuries as it became more and more the focus of monastic life at the expense of the cloister ranges.*

though the Cistercians were slow to follow them. Follow them they did, however, and by the late fourteenth century it was to the infirmary they came to eat meat. The fourteenth century saw the building of a fine meat kitchen to the south-east of the infirmary hall with two great fireplaces and a battery of ovens.

From the late fifteenth century, the aisles of the infirmary hall were divided into a series of private apartments by stone walls, providing what must have been a series of studies and bedrooms. These rooms were on two floors, evidenced by traces of staircases to the upper

floor and by latrine shafts that did not serve the ground-floor rooms in every case. Many of the rooms at ground-floor level had fireplaces. It is normally presumed that these rooms were for the sick and old, and they have been observed at Kirkstall and Waverley as well as at Fountains. However, a similar provision can be found at Byland where the infirmary was swept away in the later Middle Ages and replaced by a similar series of cells built from reclaimed materials. It would seem at both Byland and Fountains groups of monks had left the cloister for more comfortable accommodation.

John Darnton provided the infirmary with a meat refectory or misericord in the late fifteenth century, replacing an earlier building with latrines, and connected by a covered passage to the abbot's house. Little now remains of this building, but when it was excavated in the

59 *A pewter plate found among rubbish dumped outside the misericord marked with a single horseshoe to demonstrate that it was the property of the abbey.*

room served the convent as a small and comfortable dining room. Among the rubbish thrown out from it was a pewter plate, part of the garnish that must have occupied a dresser in the room (**59**).

1850s it was found to resemble a domestic hall with a raised dais at its west end and a service passage at its east end. The dais and floor were tiled and stone benches were placed along the side walls. A further wall-bench was provided on the dais which was edged with limestone blocks decorated with small quatrefoils. This

The growth of the abbot's house

As the comfort of the choir-monks increased so did that of the abbot. His house, originally of modest proportions was to grow substantially from the fourteenth century until it reached its greatest extent in the early sixteenth century (**60**).

THE SOFTENING OF CISTERCIAN IDEALS

A GROUND FLOOR

B FIRST FLOOR

The growth of the abbot's house reflected the growth of his status both within and outside the monastery. Within the abbey, the abbot was, according to the rule of St Benedict that the Cistercians followed, 'considered to represent the person of Christ' and was to be treated accordingly. As head of the community, he had obligations outside the monastery, for the abbey had extensive estates and thus feudal responsibilities. The abbot of Fountains effectively enjoyed the status of an earl and as such could be summoned to Parliament. The first abbot to be so called was Robert Thornton between 1290 and 1296. The abbot was also likely to be called on to serve on commissions for the peace of his county and to collect taxes imposed by the crown on ecclesiastical property. On the abbey's own estates he was responsible for the administration of justice. From the fourteenth century, the abbot of Fountains had additional external responsibilities as a mitred abbot, one of only three Cistercian abbots to be so honoured in England by the Pope. The granting of the mitre, ring, gloves and sandals, the insignia of a bishop, was only made to the heads of religious houses who were important and sufficiently wealthy to pay for such an honour. The honour also brought quasi-episcopal jurisdiction over a whole district and a seat in the House of Lords as one of the lords spiritual. It was not a mark of monastic spirituality but a recognition of high status within the church and outside. That status was marked at Fountains by a steady growth in the size of the abbot's household and the space given over to house it.

The earliest alterations appear to belong to the time of Abbot Walter Coxwold (1316–36), who substantially modified the twelfth-century accommodation. At ground-floor level he provided a series of prison cells with their own latrines (61), accessible from the yard that lay between the infirmary cloister and the abbot's house, and from the abbot's hall by a newel stair that Coxwold added to the north wall of his house. Each had an iron staple fixed in the floor for the prisoner's chains, showing that monastic discipline could be, and was, strictly

60 A: the surviving remains of the abbot's house at ground-floor level; B: the likely arrangement of the abbot's apartments at first-floor level in the early sixteenth century.

enforced. When the southernmost cell was excavated in the mid-nineteenth century, Walbran found the words *vale libertas* (farewell liberty) scratched into the wall. A Latin inscription would suggest that the prison was used for monks rather than common felons.

The accommodation at first-floor level was substantially enlarged. The wall dividing the original hall and chamber was removed to create a new hall 16.2m (53ft) long and 10m (32ft 9in) wide. The northernmost 3m (10ft) comprised the screens passage, covering an entrance in the north wall and the new spiral stair to the cells in the basement. This new hall was further improved by the addition of a wall fireplace at the south end of its east wall, the base of its stack surviving against the east wall of the house where it blocks a twelfth-century door at ground-floor level. A new chamber was created within the eastern end of the monks' latrine block, 10m (32ft 9in) square, with a latrine in its south-east corner discharging into the Skell. Later remodelling has removed virtually all trace of the fourteenth-century arrangements of this room. The scale of this enlarged abbot's house can be gauged by comparing it with the contemporary abbot's house at Jervaulx. There the complete lodging measured only 12.6m by 5.4m (41ft by 18ft), small enough to fit within the abbot of Fountains' hall, though Jervaulx was far from being a poor house. It was, however, a daughter-house of Byland, and therefore of secondary status.

Later in the fourteenth century, perhaps during the abbacy of William Gower, the abbot's house was again extended in a rather unusual way. An upper storey was added to the infirmary cloister which required the partial blocking of the open arcades at ground-floor level and the addition of new, deeper buttresses. Access to this new upper gallery was provided from the landing outside the door in the north wall of the abbot's hall. What purpose it served is uncertain, though the northern corridor might have led to a pew constructed on the cill of the southern window in the south gable of the Chapel of Nine Altars from which the abbot could hear services conducted in the southern chapel there. A bridge from the western arm of the gallery led to the area over the chapter-house which had originally formed a part of the dormitory, and it was here that a private chapel was created for the abbot. A new

window was inserted into the centre of the east wall of this room in the late fourteenth century.

It was Marmaduke Huby who was responsible for the final remodelling of the house, though little of his building work remains. Excavation in the nineteenth century recovered the remains of fine square-headed windows that had lit his rooms. A limestone panel of the Annunciation of the Virgin, removed from the site in the eighteenth century (**62**) is so similar to that over the door to the abbot's house at Rievaulx that it probably occupied a similar position here. Excavation also recovered 'stones bearing the well-known initials MH', none of which can now be identified, but a similar panel from an overmantel (**63**) was also recovered from a local cottage and most probably came from the abbot's house. Work of Huby's time can be recognized in the basement of his great chamber at the south end of the house to which oriel windows were added, and in the infirmary cloister. Here great chimneys and latrine towers were added to both sides of the passage, and the fourteenth-century upper storey must have been substantially rebuilt. It had become a long gallery where the abbot and his guests could exercise indoors, an addition that was becoming fashionable in the greatest of private houses. To the north of the gallery remains the ground floor of a two-storey building that housed the abbot's secretariat, Huby's *nova camera versus ecclessiam* or 'church chamber' where so many of his leases were witnessed.

Though Marmaduke Huby was known in his lifetime as a reformer, the extent of his building works and those of his predecessors indicates how far Cistercian life had moved in four centuries. It was only the reformation of the English church in the 1530s that stopped the continuing development of Fountains, preserving so well the form of twelfth- and thirteenth-century buildings which were already becoming redundant.

61 *(Above left) The basement level of the abbot's house as it survives today contains on its west side the remains of three prison cells each with its own latrine.*

62 *(Below left) A limestone panel depicting the Annunciation of the Virgin. It shows the Virgin standing to the right next to a reading desk with a cranked stem, with a vase of lilies at the centre, and the archangel Gabriel kneeling to the left. The scroll reads* AVE M(A)RI(A) (GRACIA) PLENA D(OMI)N(U)S TECU(M) *(Hail Mary, full of grace, the Lord be with you). A similar panel is set over the door to the abbot's house at Rievaulx and this panel probably occupied a similar position at Fountains.*

63 *Part of the overmantle of a highly decorative fireplace, this stone bears the device of Marmaduke Huby. The initials* m h *flank a crozier set within a mitre and are composed of intertwined biting dragons except for the upright stem of the* h *which is a hobby or small hawk that puns on the abbot's name. Above is a scroll that would have originally been painted with the words 'Soli Deo Honor et Gloria'.*

5

Agriculture, industry and wealth

Fountains, in common with the majority of medieval monasteries, depended on an agricultural and industrial estate for the support of the community and the financing of its building campaigns. Exceptionally, Archbishop Thurstan had omitted to provide the substantial landed endowment that normally accompanied the foundation of a religious house, and the monks were therefore obliged to build up an estate as best they could. Their success in this venture was one of the most remarkable in the history of the monastic church.

The nature and extent of the estate

At the foundation, Serlo tells us that Archbishop Thurstan provided the community with two carucates (about 105ha or 260 acres) of cultivated land at Sutton to the north of Ripon and 81ha (200 acres) in the wood of Herleshowe to the south of the abbey for their support. Some of this land was actually the gift of the archbishop's tenant Wallef FitzArkill, and Thurstan was doing little more than confirming that gift. From that small and inadequate beginning, it was only the monks' reputation for strict and spiritual living and their abbots' administrative skills that were to persuade the land-owning classes to grant them lands for their sustenance. In the earliest years, when failure seemed likely, they were initially reluctant to part even with moorland that was marginal to their own estates. Once established, however, it was a different story, with the great northern families, the Mowbrays, the Percys, the Romellis and the Earls of Richmond vying to surpass each others' generosity. Although the abbey estates were broken up in the 1540s it is possible to reconstruct their extent from a number of sources, starting in the last years of the abbey's life and working backwards (**64**).

Two surviving documents are central to understanding the nature and extent of Fountains' landholdings: a collection of the abbey's charters and confirmations made for Marmaduke Huby in the last years of the fifteenth century bound up in five volumes, four of which survive – the details of the missing volume can be recovered from an earlier cartulary; and the survey of the monastery's income made in 1535 for the *Valor Ecclesiasticus* (see Chapter 6). Taken together, an impressive picture can be reconstructed of the lands owned by the abbey and their respective values in the late Middle Ages. In all, Fountains had an interest in some 138 vills, ranging from the holding of a single tenement to the whole of the manor. In 1535, the taxable income of these individual holdings ranged from 1s (5p) to £111 6s 8d (£111.33), and the total net taxable income of the estate was some £1115, making Fountains the richest house of the order in England. Fountains' income had grown to four times that of its rival Rievaulx.

The Cistercian approach to estate management

From their earliest years, the Cistercians rejected the normal sources of monastic revenue: churches with their tithes, manors held by feudal tenure, mills and rents, for these did not 'accord with monastic purity' and contact with laymen distracted the monks from their devotions. Instead, they chose to accept the gifts of land that they could directly manage themselves with great armies of lay brothers who were subject to monastic discipline. Yorkshire in the twelfth century was ideal territory for

64 *The landholdings of Fountains Abbey.*
For the most part the abbey's estates lay in
Yorkshire, though there were also substantial
holdings in Cumbria. Many of the symbols
on this map conceal substantial holdings.
The granges are 1 Aldburgh; 2 Arnford;
3 Baldersby; 4 Bradley; 5 Bramley; 6 Brimham;
7 Bouthwaite; 8 Bordley; 9 Busby; 10 Cowton;
11 Dacre; 12 Eston; 13 Galphay; 14 Heyshaw;
15 Kilnsey; 16 Kirby Wiske; 17 Malham;
18 Marston; 19 Marton; 20 Nutwith; 21 Pott;
22 Sawley; 23 Sutton; 24 Thorpe Underwood;
25 Wheldrake.

Cistercian expansion. The Yorkshire Domes-
day survey of 1086 shows that out of 1500
villages in the county 850 were totally depopulated and a further 400 had severely reduced
populations due to the Danish raids that followed the conquest of England in 1066 and
King William's harrying of the north after
abortive rebellions. The precise situation is still
far from understood and the population of the
county must have begun to recover before
1130, but it is fair to assume that large parts
of Yorkshire and particularly the marginal
uplands were still substantially under-
populated. For an order which sought isolation
from the world this was an ideal situation.

The key to Cistercian land-management was the grange or estate centre which might lie at a considerable distance from the abbey and which provided a focus for a particular block of land. Staffed by lay brothers, it was a self-contained unit supported by outlying lodges and could exploit a mixed economy. Granges, like the abbeys of the order, were required to be in unpopulated areas to prevent 'contamination' from the outside world. This helped the Cistercians to maintain their policy of centralized farming which cut across the traditional (and less efficient) agricultural economy of the countryside. Where the local arrangements did not suit this method existing populations would be ruthlessly evicted if they got in the way of the grange system. It was not a policy that made the Cistercians popular though it added to their wealth, and Fountains was no exception, depopulating the vills of Cayton, Greenberry and Thorpe Underwood to create estate centres. Some granges had specialist functions, for instance the breeding of horses and cattle. Others were the centres of great sheep-runs or were industrial in nature. They functioned as a network, one communicating with another, and all communicating with the abbey at the centre. The concept was remarkably simple and highly centralized, depending for its success on the right grants of land from patrons and a good supply of well-motivated lay brothers. In the twelfth century both were freely available, and enabled the order to exploit land in a way which had not been possible since the last years of the Roman empire. Indeed, the model for this approach could have been the Roman Imperial estates themselves.

No medieval buildings survive today on any of the Fountains granges except for chapels at Bewerley and Morcar, and only one, Cowton Grange, has been excavated. There, substantial timber-framed buildings on cobbled footings had been replaced by smaller-scale domestic buildings in the fourteenth century. However, there are pointers to the nature of early Cistercian granges in England. At Laskill, a home grange of Rievaulx, traces remain of a great stone building with evidence for a vaulted ground floor, every bit as substantial as the cloister ranges of the abbey, built perhaps in the 1160s making it contemporary with the core buildings of the monastery itself. Being out-stations for the lay brothers it would be reasonable to expect the distant granges to resemble miniature monasteries with living accommodation and a chapel as well as barns, storehouses, animal-houses and industrial buildings. The Fountains grange of Malham had a piped water supply similar to that of the monastery itself installed before 1190–1210 which implies a high degree of organization. In France, that degree of organization can still be seen in surviving buildings such as the Chaalis granges of Vaulerent and Fourcheret and the Pontigny granges of le Beugnon, Crecy and Villiers-la-Grange. In England, the principal survivor is the vast barn on the Beaulieu grange of Great Coxwell. A grange or supporting lodge was not simply a group of buildings, but also the infrastructure of arable fields, meadow, pasture and woodland, substantial traces of which remain today. In upland Yorkshire, the Fountains lay brothers substantially altered the twelfth-century landscape and much of it remains in the state they left it.

The early Cistercians went about their estate management with the same certainty that they conducted their spiritual lives. The self-confidence with which they exploited marginal land and developed its administration made them both agricultural and industrial innovators. It comes as no surprise to find that their libraries contained books on agriculture such as the twelfth-century copy of Palladius' *Opus Agriculture* that belonged to Byland Abbey and still survives. The success of the order, and the wealth that provided its monumental buildings, resulted directly from the way they exploited their estates. The ability of an abbey to attract land-grants in its formative years and the election of abbots who were skilful administrators as well as spiritual leaders would together ensure that the house developed and sustained a sound economy and guaranteed its survival and its undisturbed round of prayer. This was the secret of Fountains' success in the twelfth and early thirteenth centuries.

The development of the estate and its exploitation

After the recorded gifts of the founder Archbishop Thurstan, the first indication of the development of the abbey's estates is found in a confirmation of land gifts acknowledged by King Stephen in 1135 at the point at which the abbey was about to achieve *stabilitas*. At that stage the abbey held Thurstan's gifts of Sutton

1 The ruins of Fountains Abbey as they exist today (English Heritage).

2 A contemporary illustration of Abbot Stephen Harding *(right)* presenting his church of Cîteaux to the Virgin. On the left is the abbot of St Vaase. Both are dressed in the unbleached white habit of the early Cistercians (Bibliothèque Municipale, Dijon).

ahere mm
pluref inta
of ante se m
ua oms quos
nendof inue-
p se omne ho-
e innumera
tt cu oms tu-
iptt. cu corda
beatuf iob q
e mire diffe
a extolli p
tu dni destru-

VIA CON TRA

VERITATIS VERBA
in allegatione deficiunt sepe etia nota

3 *(Above)* A lay brother, tonsured like a monk but wearing a brown habit, cutting corn with a sickle. From an initial letter from the *Moralia in Job,* written at Cîteaux during Stephen Harding's time. (Bibliothèque Municipale, Dijon).

VA VIS

4 *(Right)* A Cistercian monk in his white habit praying at the feet of an archangel, from the *Moralia in Job*. (Bibliothèque Municipale, Dijon).

IN PROLIXO OPERE ESSE
culpabilis stili mutabilitas n deber-
ne quis tam me ex locutionis mee
immutatione reprehendat in eptali

5 St Bernard of Clairvaux inspired by God (the hand from the cloud) with two
pupils at his feet, as he was perceived by an early thirteenth-century English
Cistercian (Bodleian Library, Oxford).

6 The late twelfth-century nave which contained the lay brothers' choir is little altered since it was built and it retains large areas of its original painting. Only the west window inserted in 1494 would not be recognized by its original builders (author).

7 The masonry pattern of the wall-painting at Fountains is rarely relieved by other patterns. In the window-splays of the refectory geometric designs that perhaps reflect the pattern of the grisaille glass have been recorded (Keith Emerick).

8 *(Above)* William Richardson's view of the choir and presbytery before they were cleared of fallen masonry in the middle of the nineteenth century shows clearly the contrast between the twelfth- and thirteenth-century work in the church.

10 *(Above)* An artist's reconstruction of the Chapel of Nine Altars after its repair and re-roofing by John Darnton in the 1480s (Alan Sorrell).

9 *(Left)* A mosaic pavement of geometric patterns in the south transept of Byland Abbey gives an excellent impression of the appearance of John of Kent's *pictum pavimentum* laid in the presbytery and Nine Altars at Fountains (Jim Lang).

11 A bench end carved by the Bromfletes of Ripon for Jervaulx Abbey in the 1520s. Abbot Huby's choir-stalls would have been of similar quality (Stuart Harrison).

12 John Aislabie's avenue in the park at Studley was focused on the great minster church at Ripon, a landscape feature like Fountains Abbey that he did not need to own to enjoy, painted by Balthazar Nebot in about 1760 (National Trust).

and Herleshowe, and two carucates at Cayton in two parcels of land, the gift of Eustace FitzJohn of Knaresborough. A second confirmation issued by Stephen before 1152 and after Thurstan's death in 1140, the period which saw the building and rebuilding of the permanent buildings of the monastery, unhelpfully gives no details of the lands granted from the York archiepiscopal estates by Henry Murdac, and by Alan Earl of Richmond and other faithful barons. For the growth of the abbey estates in that critical period we have to look elsewhere. A confirmation of Pope Eugenius issued in 1146, lists granges at Sutton, Cayton, Cowton Moor, Warsill, Dacre and Aldburgh, in addition to further lands in Rainborough, New Hall and Troutsdale as well as those lands given by Eustace FitzJohn 'for the building of the abbey'. A similar grant, known only from the cartulary, was made by Adam FitzSwain in 1145. The building of permanent stone ranges for the monks was thus paralleled by the organization of the abbey's landholdings into the basis of a fully developed grange structure and perhaps Henry Murdac's hand should be seen in this.

From existing charters, most of which are remarkably difficult to date accurately, it is possible to see how the estates were assembled from many individual grants. The two principal periods of acquisition appear to be in the late 1140s and 1150s and from 1174 to 1185. Amongst the earliest were those of Robert de Sartis and his wife Raganild who gave lands in Bishop Thornton for an annual rent of 6s 8d (33p) and who sold the monks Gill Moor where they had established a sheep-run before 1136. That land was not an outright gift indicates that the convent was seeking land rather than simply being given it and at such an early date when the convent was in no position to fund its own purchases, some of the earliest donations must have been of cash. Robert and his wife also rented land at Warsill to the convent for half a mark of silver (33p) which they later gave the community and which was coupled with the grant of three carucates at Herleshowe. The land at Warsill remained until 1539 the basis of the early grange there: 195 ha (482 acres) of pasture, meadow and woods.

More complex was the assembly of lands in Nidderdale to the south and west of the abbey. Bertram Haget, the father of the later Abbot Ralph and a tenant of the Mowbrays, gave the community lands valued at two marks (£1.33), a substantial holding when compared to the 195 ha (482 acres) at Warsill, on which the grange of Dacre was established as early as 1138. Some years later, Roger de Mowbray, the most generous of Fountains' benefactors and the founder of Byland Abbey, added to his tenant's grant and allowed the grange to be relocated on better land that he had farmed himself. He also gave the mineral rights in the forest of Nidderdale to the monks, and in 1174 granted the convent the greater part of the forest itself. In 1175 he further added to the monks' holdings in Nidderdale. In the same year he lost a substantial part of his estates as a result of his involvement in an abortive rebellion against King Henry II. As a result, Fountains lost the lands held from Roger south of Dacre. Roger was obliged to compensate the monks by granting additional land (for a payment) at Dallow Moor on the east side of Nidderdale and a few days later all of his holding at Lofthouse. Earl Roger's disgrace was to Fountains' advantage, for having lost royal favour he judged it wise to leave the kingdom and go on pilgrimage to Jerusalem. This was an expensive business and Roger turned to Fountains for assistance, selling the abbey land to the value of £450. Though there is no evidence that he actually went to Jerusalem at the time, he was later to go on crusade and die a captive of the Saracens in 1188. By the end of the twelfth century, the greater part of upper Nidderdale was in the abbey's hands.

From William de Percy came vast estates in Craven granted before 1174. This included all of the pasture of Malham Moor, and Malham Tarn with its important fishery, William's tenants Thurstan de Arches and Ulf FitzRoskill provided further grants of land around Malham, making this area a major estate in its own right. His daughter Matilda, Countess of Warwick, continued her father's benefaction, giving further lands in Malham and the forest of Langstroth, to which her sister and co-heiress Agnes, wife of Jocelin de Louvain, added. Later Percys were to regret the munificence of their forebears and were to challenge unsuccessfully Fountains' rights to many estates in the courts. The outcome of these disputes was that Fountains' holdings were confirmed and further endowments were offered. Richard de Percy, as a grant to persuade the monks to accept his body for burial in the mid-thirteenth century, gave the abbey the whole vill of Litton in Craven with the forest of Littondale, an area which had been in dispute for three generations. Richard's son Henry disputed this settlement, and it was not until 1297 and the payment of 600 marks of silver by the abbey, that Fountains had secure title to this land. It can be seen from the surviving agreements and court rolls that the building up of so extensive an estate was both slow and complicated, requiring so great an overview that the abbey must have been working to a blueprint from its earliest years.

Between 1203 and 1265, a considerable effort was made to consolidate the abbey's lands, renting out areas that were not easily farmed in hand and acquiring parcels of land that complemented areas already held, either by exchange or purchase. Agreements were reached with both Rievaulx and Byland that neither would act to the disadvantage of Fountains as they carried out the same exercise, and with other monasteries where it was felt necessary. Such prior agreement did not always work and Fountains found itself having to take legal action against other monks to protect its interests. Such was the competition for land that Fountains found itself accusing the abbot and convent of Furness of forgery and perjury in their attempt to secure disputed holdings in Craven in the early fourteenth century. Fountains was not above dubious practice either, for at the end of the thirteenth century the monks enclosed a highway at Wheldrake that prevented access to land held by Warter Priory there. In this case Fountains was forced to make amends and provide a new road. The resulting agreement shows that the canons of Warter held a deep mistrust of the Fountains monks which resulted from a history of high-handedness. The same slackening in Cistercian life that was noted in the conventual buildings can be seen in the monks' attitude to farming and estate management.

By 1265, the Fountains holdings had reached their maximum extent and represented a highly organized and profitable estate that was not entirely confined to Yorkshire. There were few granges at great distance from the abbey, and all were strategically placed as staging-posts to link distant holdings with the abbey itself. In this way, the grange of Baldersby to the north-east of Fountains provided the first link in the chain of estate centres that ran through Kirkby Wiske to Cowton in the Vale of Mowbray and Busby in Cleveland. Similarly, Marton and Thorpe Underwood were stages on the journey to York and the important grange of Wheldrake on the Derwent, a route which also passed through Hammerton and Marston. Substantial though the landholdings to the east were, the main body of the Fountains lands lay on the higher ground to the west, extending in a virtually unbroken sweep from the west gates of the abbey into Lancashire and Cumberland.

To the north of the abbey were the home granges of Swanley, Galphay and Sutton, to the south-west Warsill, and to the south Morker (or Herleshowe), Haddockstanes and Cayton. Beyond these, further granges were set on the floor of the dales that reach up into the Pennines. Lower Wensleydale was managed from Sleningford, while the upper reaches were administered from Aldburgh and Nutwith. Pott grange lay on the flank of Colsterdale, and Bramley at the headwaters of the river Laver. Lower Nidderdale was served by Dacre and the lodges of Brimham, Bewerley and Heyshaw, and the upper dale by Bouthwaite and the lodge of Lofthouse. Huge tracts of land on the east side of the dale were held by Fountains on Dallow Moor and Fountains Earth Moor above Bouthwaite grange. Kilnsey served upper Wharfedale and Arncliffe served Littondale. These granges were serviced by the lodges of Foxup, Cosh, Upper and Lower Heseldon and Fornagill which were tucked into the narrow ghylls that provided access to the high moors. Fountains Fell on the south flank of Pen-y-Ghent bears testimony to the abbey's sheep runs there. Malham and the twin granges of Bordley lay in Craven, off the headwaters of Airedale, with Arnfold planted in Ribblesdale, controlling vast areas of pasture and arable land. Malham Moor was good sheep and cattle territory, and the abbey's *bercariae* and *vaccariae* with their pastures, droves, buildings and animal-pens can still be traced in the earthworks that extend across the landscape there (**65**).

65 *The earthwork remains of Bolton Priory's bercary on Abbot Hills above Malham, a property disputed with Fountains, lie at the centre of extensive grazing enclosures. Fountains' own ranches in the area differ little in their layout* (Steve Moorhouse).

Large grazing enclosure

Large grazing enclosure

Large grazing enclosure

M

?B

M

M

?B

Site of buildings

Tumbled walling: buildings
Tumbled walling: enclosures
Probable wall line
Assumed wall line
Edge of tabular limestone
Edge of tabular limestone forming boundary to site
Artificial slope
Entrance
B   Blocking
M   Mole-infested area

0 10 20 30 40 50 60 70 80 90 100 metres

N

SAM 1987

66 *The lands of Bradley Grange can be reconstructed from charter evidence. K marks the site of the Kirklees Priory mill, F1 the proposed site of the Fountains mill, F2 its final location, P the site of the Upper Heaton pottery making site, and* I *the ironworks of* Smytheclough (Steve Moorhouse).

Only two granges lay outside this closely woven net, Bradley near Huddersfield on the Calder, and Allerdale in Cumberland. From these far-flung estates wayleaves had been negotiated for the moving of stock over other people's land. At Bradley, a holding of some 1780ha (4400 acres) had been assembled in the late twelfth century. The grange was established by 1193 and by 1194 the abbey was operating a forge there producing iron. Bradley was made up of a series of small grants in the townships of Huddersfield and Kirkheaton, the extents of which can be ascertained from surviving charter evidence (**66**). There is evidence to suggest that Fountains had targeted the area because of its industrial potential, and as parcels of land were acquired, wayleaves between them were negotiated in a way which suggests the monks were acting to a masterplan that would give them access to iron ore, timber and watercourses, all essential if a forge was to be established. The monks of Rievaulx were acquiring similar provisions at Flockton and Wombwell in the 1160s and 1170s, as was Byland at its granges of Bentley and Denby. As well as being pioneers of agriculture, the Cistercians were also in the forefront of industrial development. They were not alone in this endeavour, for at the same period the important Augustinian house of Gisborough was developing its ironworks in Eskdale. The production of iron was a highly profitable venture.

At Bradley, evidence for ironworking survives in the largely rural area of Kirkheaton in the valley of *Smythclough* where substantial earthworks and scatters of ironworking debris and slag indicate the site of perhaps the earliest identified water-powered industrial complex in medieval England. Bradley's economy was not, however, predominantly industrial, although it does include a pottery production site of the thirteenth and fourteenth centuries at Upper (or Potter) Heaton where monastic exploitation of a traditionally peasant industry to serve the Fountains properties in this part of West Yorkshire can be assumed. The grange also had cattle and sheep, and the presence of a mill implies extensive arable farming. The mill itself has a remarkable history which is perhaps typical of the problems that even major monasteries faced in organizing their estates. Fountains had entered into a series of agreements with its neighbours in order that they might build a mill on the river Calder. The poor nuns of Kirklees, themselves Cistercian, controlled the north bank of the Calder and built their own mill above the Fountains site, depriving the proposed mill of an uninterrupted water supply. Although Fountains had shown itself to be willing in other cases to use its might to overawe lesser houses, in this case the monks seem to have been unwilling to take on the prioress of Kirklees and chose instead to build their mill on the Colne where they controlled both banks of the river.

In the twelfth and thirteenth centuries, Fountains' income was substantially derived from the wool-trade, using the proceeds to finance buildings, both within the precinct and on the granges and lodges, and to buy land (which the community was technically forbidden to do by the statutes of the order). By 1300, the abbey ran some 15,000 sheep and revenue from the sale of wool was three times that from all other sources. The wool-trade has tended to overshadow the abbey's other interests which were as extensive as they were varied. There were substantial fisheries on Derwentwater and Malham Tarn, on the rivers Swale and Wiske, on the rivers Ure and Ouse between Boroughbridge and York, and on the river Derwent at Wheldrake. Several granges also practised fish-culture, their ponds still being traceable. Sea-fishing was practised off Teesmouth. They had resources to meet other needs too. Stone slates for roofing and stone for building were quarried in Craven, Nidderdale, Skelldale and on Hutton Moor. Millstones were similarly quarried and worked at Sawley and at Crossland near Huddersfield. Lead and iron were mined and refined in Nidderdale, and timber for fuel and for building was available across the estate.

Urban properties

Although the General Chapter of the order had ruled in 1134 that monks were not to live in towns, this does not seem to have particularly bothered the Fountains monks who were assembling urban properties of varying extent in the towns of Boston, Yarm, Grimsby, Scarborough, York, Ripon and Doncaster. With the exception of the last two, all the towns targeted were ports and the purpose of establishing a presence there was trade, as the abbey practised a surplus economy. Boston and York were the principal ports for the export of wool first to Flanders and later to Italy, and the abbey's involvement there is understandable. Holdings in Grimsby, Scarborough, Redcar and Yarm provided access to the markets there, particularly for the purchase of sea-fish that made up a substantial element of the monks' diet.

In Boston, the principal property lay in Wormgate where it is still marked by Fountain Lane. It was primarily used during the great fair of St Botulph as the headquarters of the abbey's agents. First granted before 1200 by Jordan de Boston, it was gradually expanded during the first half of the thirteenth century to include two mills in an area of land called *le poll*. A second property lay in Emery Lane on the west bank of the river Witham, adjacent to a property held by the prior of Thornholme who acted as an agent for many of the small

67 *Pottery from the kiln-site at Winklsey. As well as decorated jugs, the Winksley potters were also making cooking pots and bowls, and roof-tiles for the abbey buildings* (Jean le Patourel).

Lincolnshire monasteries in the wool-trade. It was enlarged by the acquisition of a second tenement in 1248. The bulk of Fountains' urban property was in York where acquisition began in the 1170s and included a house with a resident caretaker and cook to provide for the officers of the monastery when they were in the city on business. The York properties were mainly on land close to the river and were so organized as to provide a major outlet for the abbey's wool exports. In 1224, the abbey owned its own ship licensed to carry wool, a privilege shared with the daughter-house of Kirkstall that indicates the level of investment made in the wool-trade. Properties not so well placed in York were leased out for a cash income.

The home granges

The abbey itself was ringed by a series of home granges whose purpose was to provide a focus for the more distant estates. They were principally the first granges to be established, with one important exception. They conducted the business that was either too noisy or unpleasant to be carried out within the precinct itself, and they contained the animal-houses and barns that would be found within the precinct of a less important abbey. They also acted as home-farms producing the convent's immediate food needs. To the north of Fountains lay Sutton Grange, based on Thurstan's first gift of land and a grange by 1146. Roger de Mowbray and his tenants gave additional lands and before 1156 the monks were keeping cattle there. By 1185 the grange had achieved the extent recorded by the suppression commissioners in 1539, lying astride the Kex Beck over which the monks had two bridges. Within the grange, the monks established a major pottery production site at Winksley in the late twelfth century.

Four kilns have been excavated and large quantities of the pottery produced have been recovered (**67**). This pottery has an interesting distribution, being extremely rare in the market town of Ripon which is only 6.4 km (4 miles) away and where it could have been marketed if it was produced for sale. Instead, it is found predominantly to the south and west of the kiln-site and particularly at Fountains Abbey itself. The pottery produced is distinctive, for while the forms and fabrics used are derived from those of the contemporary Scarborough pottery industry, the wedge-shaped rouletted decoration is copied from the Dutch pottery industry at Aardenburg. The Winksley kilns were established to serve the abbey and its home granges, yet a further example of the self-sufficiency of the Cistercian grange system. The kilns remained in production until the last quarter of the thirteenth century, producing not only pottery but roof-tiles as well, which were certainly used on the abbey's buildings.

To the south of the abbey lay two extensive granges, those of Morker and Haddockstanes. The earthworks of the central enclosure of Morker remain at Nineveh Farm on the south side of the abbey precinct and the remains of a wall can still be seen along the western boundary of the grange. A gate in the precinct wall provided access from the grange to the Outer Court of the abbey. Between the grange buildings and the precinct wall were between 1 and 2 ha (some 4 acres) of fishponds and there is slight evidence of extensive stock compounds. To the west and enclosed by the 'Monks' Wall' was the grange of Haddockstanes extending as far north as the south bank of the river Skell. To the south of both lay Warsill, providing Fountains with a substantial farming capacity. Haddockstanes included part of the wood of Herleshowe and the surviving chapel of St Michael on Howe Hill. It also included a massive complex of four groups of fishponds covering 16 ha (40 acres) at Park House Farm. When these were recorded in the late 1950s by Roy Gilyard-Beer, each group of ponds had the associated earthworks of a stone-built smoke-house for the curing of fish. Only one group of ponds now remains in a recognizable state, but the degree of organization is still apparent.

Perhaps the most remarkable of the home granges was that of Swanley adjoining the abbey precinct on the north. As with most other estates it had been assembled from a series of grants but here the process of assembly belongs to the thirteenth and not the twelfth century. Alan de Aldfield acknowledged the gifts of his ancestors and granted a further area of land in 1272, providing the abbey with a block of land that stretched from the brow of the hill overlooking the abbey on its north down to the river Skell. The grants concern land in the present-day parishes of Aldfield and Lindrick with Studley Royal and Fountains, from the valley of the Keldal to the north to the precinct wall of the abbey and the river to the south, and from the parish boundary of Aldfield to the west to

68 *The grange at Swanley can be reconstructed from its land-grants which remained identifiable as fields on the tithe map of 1844 (after Judith Roebuck with additions).*

the Skell valley on the east (**68**). It comprised the same 58 ha (144 acres) in 1535: 14 ha (35 acres) of arable land; 12 ha (30 acres) of pasture; and 11 ha (28 acres) of meadow. The remaining 21 ha (51 acres) must have comprised buildings, animal-pens and woodland. The land was not formally farmed as a grange before 1300 but a confirmation of the earlier gifts of land by John de Mowbray in April 1317 provides a likely date for its inception.

The early fourteenth century was a troubled time for the abbey, for the disastrous defeat of the English at Bannockburn had left the north of England open to Scottish raiding to the extent that the walled city and castle of York were felt to be insecure. In 1318, many of the Fountains estates were overrun by the Scots, their buildings burned and contents looted, and the general spirit of lawlessness that pervaded the north made recovery difficult. The supply of lay brothers had also been reduced to a trickle, and the abbey was forced to reconsider the way it managed its estates. The means chosen required the removal of some activities from granges that were no longer directly farmed which were to be brought into the abbey itself.

As the Fountains precinct was small 30 ha (74 acres) compared with the 40.4 ha (100 acres) of Rievaulx), the development of an additional home grange in the early fourteenth century seems to have been the answer, and there can be little surprise that Swanley Grange was connected to the Inner Court of the monastery by a road that can still be observed above the Inner Gatehouse.

The economy of Fountains in the later Middle Ages

Deprived of lay brothers, Fountains was no longer able to consider farming its estates in hand, and three options were open to the convent. The granges could be run by hired workmen under the control of a bailiff, they could be leased to secular tenants, or depopulated vills could be repopulated and farmed on a feudal basis. Each option was counter to the twelfth-century statutes and would compromise the very centralization that had made the abbey so powerful. Times had changed, though, and Fountains was not alone in being faced with the need to reform its economy. Most monasteries took the easy choice of tenanting the majority of their lands and subsisting on rents. Fountains, cushioned by its wealth, was able to take a longer view and set about a comprehensive review of its holdings and their management.

Workable granges were staffed by hired labour and remained in hand under the control of 10 bailiffs, serving Sleningfold and Galphay, Craven, Nidderdale, Stainburn, Wheldrake, Hartwith, Grantley and Dalaghy, Aldburgh, Cowton and Greenberry, and Thorpe Underwood. An eleventh bailiff was appointed to manage the Outer Court of the monastery itself. In 1336, Abbot Coxwold leased those granges damaged in the wars to tenants, but not on a simple rental basis. Leasing had been allowed by the General Chapter in 1208 and Fountains had used leases as a way of managing land that was not central to its estates from the late twelfth century. The new tenants were not free to farm the lands as they wished, and might better be described as managers for they were required to wear the abbot's livery and owed him service in a feudal manner. From the leases that survive, it is clear that the stock they farmed was the property of the abbey and if a cow died, the abbey would provide a replacement on the production of its hide, which of course was processed by the house's tannery. Tenants were required to bring their stock annually to the abbey where it was slaughtered, preventing its disposal on the open market. Finally, Abbot Robert Monkton began the conversion of granges into populated manors in 1363, effectively reversing the abbey's earlier policy of depopulation. By the early years of the fifteenth century, there was little difference between the management of Fountains' estates and those of any other major monastery.

The conversion of the estates to lay management, while it was done in a way that exerted central control, undoubtedly had a marked effect on the landscape. Many of the smaller vaccaries and bercaries were abandoned, and granges were remodelled to suit their changed management. Gone were many of the great buildings, to be replaced by smaller and more easily managed structures. At Cowton, for instance, the large timber buildings of the twelfth century were replaced by more domestic hall, chamber and kitchen of the scale more commonly found on lay manorial sites and which were more appropriate to a tenant or bailiff. The abbey itself appears to have provided these buildings, for tenancy agreements invariably contain a statement that the tenant is responsible for all repairs to the buildings but that the abbey was responsible for the provision of 'large timbers and stone thack [slates]'.

The Outer Court of the monastery

All that part of the precinct that lay on the south side of the river Skell comprised the Outer or Base Court of the monastery, an area given over to agricultural and industrial processes on which the life of the house depended (**69**). It had its own gate to the outside world, the South Gate, somewhat confusingly set in the west wall of the precinct. Today the Outer Court largely survives as earthworks, but parts of two buildings survive, the mill and the woolhouse, and a third building, the tannery existed in 1540 when the site was being offered for sale. The location of the tannery is no longer known but it is suspected to lie close to the river and to the west of the guest-house complex for it would have required a regular supply of water. Excavation in the 1880s by William St John Hope has identified a further building, the malthouse and brewhouse, to the south of the woolhouse. A study of the landscape has revealed the sites of a further 21 buildings all with associated yards and a network of roads that link them one to another. There are almost certainly more buildings that remain untraced. None of these buildings has been excavated or can be tied to documents that identify them, and there is as yet no evidence that they are all contemporary though they must all be monastic. Additionally there are large areas of land that contain no evidence of buildings but appear to have been cultivated as they bear slight evidence of ridge-and-furrow ploughing, areas of pasture for the animals that were kept within the precinct.

The Outer Court was the public area of the monastery as well as the centre of the monastic estate. There were barns and animal houses, dovecots, mills, granaries, slaughter-house, workshops, stables and industrial buildings. The convent's plumber, smith and joiners would have been based there, often with houses as well as workshops. The tannery, if it was of similar scale to that at Rievaulx, would have had an associated bark store, barn and tanner's house all set about a yard.

Women were allowed into the Outer Court, and the wife of the keeper of the south gate was laundress to the convent. If the world of the cloister was quiet and controlled, the Outer Court was very different, a hive of noisy activity that sustained the convent throughout the year. Originally the province of the lay brothers, from the fourteenth century it would

69 *The precinct of Fountains Abbey enclosed by its thirteenth-century wall and ringed by home granges. The Outer Court comprised the whole of the enclosed area to the south of the river Skell. Only surviving buildings and those that have been excavated are shown.*

have been staffed by laymen, hired servants responsible to a bailiff, many of whom would have lived in the court. At the suppression it is likely that the abbey would have had at least 150 paid servants whose duties lay outside the cloister.

The centre of 'industrial' activity was a deep ghyll that ran down the hillside with groups of buildings on terraces to the east and west, with the brewhouse and woolhouse, the latter the largest single building, at its northern end (**70**). The powerful stream that ran down the ghyll provided the power to drive small mills, and building 72 that stood astride the stream was quite possibly served by a water-wheel. To the west of the ghyll were three areas of pasture, 8, 9 and 19, each containing buildings (14, 15, 11 and 12) which were probably animal-houses or byres associated with the pasture. At some

stage the pasture had been re-divided into two areas by an earthen bank and associated road (18). To the east of the ghyll were two areas, known as East and West Applegarths in the early sixteenth century, which approximate to two areas of pasture (131 and 110). East Applegarth lay adjacent to Pondgarth, which in turn contained a series of deep tanks (140, 142 and 147) which supplied water to the cloister buildings by way of the conduit house of Robin Hood's Well. A similar tank (52) to the west of West Applegarth supplied the lay brothers' quarters with piped water. The complexity of the Outer Court is similar to that at Rievaulx where there are at least 40 buildings known from sixteenth-century surveys, and the scale of the provision is commensurate with the extent of the Fountains estates of which this area is the focus. Only excavation will reveal the true nature of the buildings which are now covered by turf. However, examination of the surviving buildings will show the scale and quality of the buildings that serviced so wealthy a monastery.

The mill is the finest surviving example of a monastic corn mill in England (**71**); it appears

70 (Above) The Outer Court is defined by a series of prominent earthworks which can be identified as the sites of buildings (shown in black outline), garths, and roadways, as well as open areas that show traces of cultivation (after RCHM).

71 (Below) The surviving mill which was operational until 1937 is one of the finest monastic water-mills in Europe.

72 *The mill in the early twelfth century (Phase 1) and mid-twelfth century (Phase 2)*

Phase 3

BASEMENT

wheel pit

WORKING FLOOR

Phase 4

break in coursing

GRANARY

pentice over

c 1135-46
inferred
c 1150-80
inferred
13th century
inferred
c 1450

metres
0 1 2 3 4 5 10

73 *The mill in the early thirteenth century (Phase 3).*

to be an early thirteenth-century building which incorporates earlier masonry. It has recently been the subject of detailed archaeological study, though it has yet to be excavated, and for the first time it is possible to disentangle its structure and identify no fewer than three distinct buildings (**72, 73** and **74**). The

earliest building, represented by its east and south walls, each with a surviving window, dated from the late 1130s or early 1140s and thus belongs to the first stone monastery. The visible masonry belongs to the upper floor of the building and survives to wall-plate level. The lower storey, which had a wheel at its south end driven by a surviving race, was buried in the 1150s when a new mill was built. This mill was set on a dam to create a mill-pond that powered an undershot wheel in the old

EAST ELEVATION: medieval masonry

WEST ELEVATION: medieval masonry

CROSS SECTION A B

SOUTH ELEVATION: medieval masonry

74 *The surviving medieval masonry of the Fountains Abbey mill, with post-medieval additions removed for clarity.*

race to the south, and a breastshot wheel at the north end of the building.

The ground floor of the first mill was buried within the dam, and the east wall of the upper floor was retained to support the east wall of the new mill, enclosing its basement and wheel-pits. The new building had single light round-headed windows and doors, though none of the windows survive. They were converted to two-light windows in the thirteenth century, one jamb coursed with the twelfth-century wall and one very clearly inserted. The early thirteenth-century rebuilding added an upper storey granary to the old mill and extended it at the north end, where it was of two rather than three storeys. Additionally, a now-lost building was built against its south-east corner in the four-teenth century. Apart from the insertion of new

75 *The woolhouse as excavated was a complicated structure with five identifiable periods of building.*

window-heads in the ground-floor windows of the west elevation and some internal partitioning in the early eighteenth century, the mill remained unaltered and in use until 1937, almost eight centuries after the first part of it was built. In its architecture, this building reflects all the significant periods of change in the abbey's economic life and its survival as a working building attests to its quality of construction. Although devoid of unnecessary decoration, the mill is architecturally distinguished, a certain pointer to its importance.

No less important was the woolhouse, a great aisled storehouse of four bays now reduced almost totally to low walling (**75**). Excavation has proved it to be a complex structure, part of a massive range of buildings that included the malthouse and brewhouse, with six principal phases of construction from its first building in the 1150s to its eventual demolition in the late fifteenth century. Essentially the woolhouse was a great barn with an office for the obedien-

tiary attached to its north-east corner. As the abbey's economy developed throughout the thirteenth century it was enlarged, and by the end of the century it had acquired a fulling mill in its western aisle powered by an undershot wheel. The malthouse and brewhouse to the south was also rebuilt at this period. The fourteenth century saw changes in the use of the complex with the insertion of dye-vats in the remains of the fulling mill and the provision of two furnaces to provide hot water. The western aisles were partitioned off and appear to have been used for the finishing of cloth. No longer was this the woolhouse but a multi-purpose structure. Its final use came in the mid-fifteenth century when it was partitioned up as workshops used for a restoration of the abbey church. Debris indicated glaziers at work in the central part of the building, while a small blacksmith's forge was created in the eastern aisle, the smith's tongs and the lead lining of his water boshes still lying in the hammer-scale on the floor. To the south of the smithy was a pit full of bronze-working debris. In the last quarter of the fifteenth century the building had outlived its usefulness because of a changing economy and it was demolished, leaving the

76 *The woolhouse as it would have appeared in the fifteenth century, looking from the east (see 77) reconstructed with the aid of fallen architectural detail* (Simon Hayfield).

malthouse standing alone. The site was simply levelled and only good walling-stone removed. Almost all the architectural detail was thrown down close to its original location, permitting an accurate reconstruction of the building to be made (**76**). Like the mill it was a distinguished building reflecting the importance of its original use.

The malthouse and brewhouse, which formed the southern continuation of the woolhouse from the early thirteenth century, was rebuilt in fine ashlar masonry in the late thirteenth century (**77**) and with the exception of the addition of an obedientiary's office to its east side in the fourteenth century remained largely unaltered until the sixteenth century. On two storeys and with three aisles at ground-floor level, it was a substantial building. Until it is re-excavated, it is not possible to be certain of its precise function, but malting appears to have been carried out on the ground floor and brewing on the upper floor, where evidence

c. 1150 - 60
c. 1220 - 47
c. 1260 - 70
later 13th cent.
c. 1320 - 40
late 15th cent.

Woolshed

Malthouse

N

0 2 4 6 8 10 Metres

0 10 20 30 Feet

77 *The woolhouse and malthouse and brew-house together comprised a substantial building under a single roof.*

survives for a piped water supply. As with all the buildings at Fountains, its scale reflects the size of the community it supported.

Because Fountains lay at the centre of a web of estates and all its granges were focused on the abbey, the Outer Court was the centre of all the economic activity that supported the monastery. If the cloister buildings were workshops of prayer, the buildings of the Outer Court were the workshops of Mammon without which the former could not have existed. It is perhaps symbolic that the cloister buildings have survived so completely when not a single grange building apart from chapels survives above ground level, and of the Outer Court buildings only the mill survived demolition in the sixteenth century. The means has been lost but the end survives in recognizable form.

97

6

Fountains Abbey since the suppression

The end of Fountains as a working abbey came within the general suppression of English monasteries on 26 November 1539. Suppression was inevitable when the government realized that it could take over the lands and wealth of monastic houses. These had become state property when Henry VIII made himself 'Supreme Head (below God) of the church in England' in 1534, though this had been effective since 1531 when Convocation had acknowledged the king as Supreme Head 'so far as the law of Christ allowed'. The beginning of the end came about because of events at Rievaulx in 1533.

The deposing of Abbot William Thirsk

Abbot Edward Kirby of Rievaulx was a conservative abbot who was unlikely to agree with the rapid changes that were occurring in the church in the early 1530s and who fell foul of the patron of his house, Sir Thomas Manners, a staunch supporter of the King's party and who was supported by Thomas Cromwell, the King's secretary. Manners sought to depose Abbot Kirby and replace him with a more sympathetic abbot who would understand the needs of both King and church in changing times. Accordingly, Manners brought an accusation of mismanagement of the abbey's assets against Kirby, who was to be examined by his peers who included the abbots of Fountains and Byland. William Thirsk of Fountains could find no fault with Kirby, presumably because the charges were not true, and though it did not stop Kirby's deposition on Cromwell's authority, William Thirsk was a marked man.

In 1535, Thomas Cromwell was instructed to make a general visitation of all monasteries, both to ascertain their wealth and to enquire into the quality of monastic life. The former

exercise produced a detailed assessment of taxable income, the *Valor Ecclesiasticus*, which established that rich pickings were to be had if the monasteries were to be dissolved, and led to the Act of Suppression of 1536 by which all monasteries with an annual income of less than £200 were to be closed down for the benefit of the Crown. Greater monasteries where 'religion was well kept' were to remain. The second survey, conducted in the north by Drs Richard Leyton and Thomas Leigh, unscrupulous individuals chosen more for their loyalty to Cromwell than their desire to reform monastic life, was to examine the morals of the enclosed. They arrived in Yorkshire in January 1536 and having made short work of St Mary's Abbey at York proceeded to Fountains where they started about Abbot Thirsk.

Within the abbey was a monk called Marmaduke Bradley, a schemer who had been in disgrace in the time of the reforming Abbot Huby but who had acquired a pardon for his crimes from Abbot Guillaume du Boisset of Cîteaux. He had inherited a valuable prebendal stall in Ripon Minster, and was seeking to advance his position both within the monastery and outside. Before Leyton and Leigh had visited, Bradley had offered Cromwell 600 marks in hard cash for the abbacy (in addition to the £1000 he would pay to the King over three years for the 'first fruits' due from his appointment). It is hardly surprising that the visitors found severe fault with Abbot Thirsk. Writing to Cromwell on 20 January, Richard Leyton described Thirsk as 'a very fool and a miserable idiot' while Bradley was 'the wisest monk within England of that order and well learned, twenty years officer and ruler of all that house, a wealthy fellow . . .'. There is evidence that Thirsk was not a prudent ruler, for he had been selling the abbey's timber without the convent's agreement, but the visitors went on to accuse him of stealing jewels from the abbey's treasury at dead of night in order to sell them, considerably under-valued, to a Cheapside goldsmith, and of keeping six whores for his own amusement. There is not the slightest evidence to substantiate these allegations, and his only crime was to be a powerful and influential conservative like Abbot Kirby at Rievaulx, but Thirsk was persuaded to resign and make way for Marmaduke Bradley. Given a generous pension (that Bradley tried to have reduced), he retired to live with his friend Adam Sedbar the abbot of Jervaulx until both men unwisely became involved with the Pilgrimage of Grace and were accordingly butchered at Tyburn.

Leyton and Leigh believed that Marmaduke Bradley, as well as being generous to their master and themselves, would be more politic and pliant than his predecessor, and would better serve the King's interest. In this they were as incorrect as they had been in their reports on Thirsk. Abbot Bradley was going to get the best deal he could for himself and his community.

The suppression of Fountains

Following the northern rising generally known as the Pilgrimage of Grace, that sought amongst other things to restore the lesser monasteries suppressed in 1536, the wealthy and powerful abbeys were plainly at risk. Bridlington and Jervaulx were seized by the King because their superiors had been involved with the rebels and had been tried and executed as traitors. They provided great wealth to the Crown and it was only a short time before the decision was taken to suppress all the remaining houses. A visitation of the greater houses beginning in January 1538 was undertaken with the intention of encouraging their 'voluntary' surrender to the King. This was a long and slow business, extending into 1540, and the turn of Fountains came in November 1539.

Abbot Bradley, his prior Thomas Kydde and 30 monks signed the deed of surrender in the chapter-house on 26 November, ending almost 408 years of uninterrupted monastic life. Bradley succeeded in having his 'first fruits' substantially reduced as he had been unable to enjoy the income of his office as he had

intended, and though he had offered to give up his prebend at Ripon on his election he had somehow managed to retain it, and was to keep it until his death in 1553. He also persuaded the suppression commissioners to provide him with an annual pension of £100. His prior was to receive £8, and the monks between £6 13s 4d (£6.66) and £5, fairly standard rates for those who were prepared to go without a fuss. The rewards to the crown were spectacular, and the commissioners could afford to be generous. The abbey's estates provided a clear revenue of more than £1100 a year and the contents of the treasury and sacristies were substantial. A list made before the suppression by Brian Higdcn, Dean of York, and Edward Kirby of Rievaulx mentions 80 copes amongst other vestments, some of cloth of gold or silver, two mitres encrusted with silver gilt decoration, two croziers with silver heads, no fewer than 22 silver chalices, rich reliquaries of St Anne, St Lawrence and the True Cross, and plate weighing at least 80,514g (2840 ounces). Additionally, the bells and all the lead from the roofs were of considerable value.

The abbey buildings were not immediately dismantled as was the norm, because Henry VIII had devised a scheme to create a new bishopric with jurisdiction over Richmondshire and parts of Lancashire. As a result the buildings were mothballed for a short period before the scheme was abandoned. This short-lived stay of execution might have kept the buildings intact but it did not mean that no damage was done. Excavation by Walbran in the 1850s indicated that many graves had been looted, although he was unable to ascertain when this had happened. The excavation in 1979 of the grave in the south transept of brother John Ripon (**78**) who died in 1524 identified graphically the sequence of events which must have happened while the church was still in royal hands. The grave slab had been lifted and broken, and the upper half of the grave cut dug out, disturbing the body, which was still at least partially articulated, to retrieve the mortuary chalice and paten that had been buried with the priest. The remains of John Ripon were then thrown back into the grave with no attempt to replace them correctly and the grave refilled. This in itself is hardly remarkable, but the next occurrence is. The grave slab was carefully relaid, though part of it had been thrown into the grave fill, and missing areas

Grave 3

Grave 3 slab

(inscription after Walbran)

0   1m

0   3ft

Grave 2

Grave 1

78 *The grave of brother John Ripon, cellarer of Fountains, who died in 1524, had been robbed and restored in 1539–40 (*Simon Hayfield*).*

were made up with plaster, which was not apparent until excavation. Such a restoration can only have taken place within the context of the church being in the care of the suppression commissioners and would imply that the looting, for once at least, was unauthorized.

The sale of the site

The King's proposal was to come to nothing, and the new diocese was given to Chester Abbey, thus preserving the remains of the Benedictine house there. Before the decision was taken to do this, Cromwell had been in

negotiations with Sir Richard Gresham to sell the abbey and its home estates, and the sale was duly completed in October 1540. The dismantling of the abbey now began, for by then window glass and lead from the stripping of Fountains were appearing in Ripon and York. Normally the lead and bells were reserved for the Crown, and Gresham accounted for the casting down and removal of lead as late as 1544, when it was being transported to Hull by way of Boroughbridge and York. Furnaces were built within the abbey church, including one in the crossing, and timber from the roofs and screens used to burn the lead and cast it into sows of approximately half a ton (**79**) for ease of shipment. Not all the lead was destined to reach the King's officials, however, and in 1544, Gresham's receiver John Hall had paid

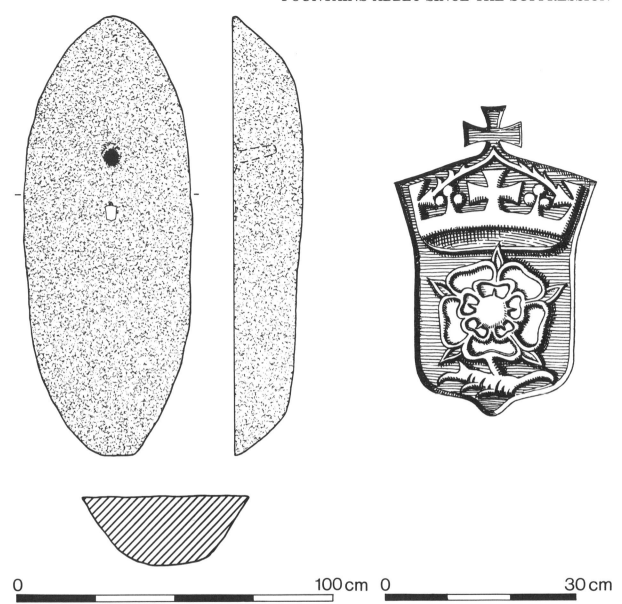

79 *A lead pig or ingot with the royal stamp recovered from the spoliation of Rievaulx Abbey. It weighs a half-fother or 9 hundredweights (G. Dunning).*

Leonard Beckwith, receiver of the Court of Augmentations which handled the receipts of former monastic estates, the sum of 8d (3p) for making an indictment against 'him that stole the leade at ffountance'.

The scale of Gresham's spoliation is difficult to ascertain, but he seems mainly to have been responsible for the unroofing of the buildings and the recovery of the King's lead, a similar exercise to that carried out by Thomas Manners at Rievaulx in 1539. There is also the possibility that it was Gresham's agents who were responsible for the partial demolition of the upper levels of the presbytery and Nine Altars, for all the decorative wall-shafts were ripped out to recover their lead packing-pieces, and the tie-rods that retained the open arcade in front of the clerestory windows were cut, ensuring that the upper works of the building collapsed fairly quickly, making the church unrestorable as the conditions of sale usually required.

The site that Gresham purchased was suitably surveyed before the sale in September 1540 by Leonard Beckwith and Hugh Fuller, and besides the church and cloister buildings, only two buildings were recorded as roofed, the corn mill that still survives and the tannery, both valuable buildings in their own right, though the tannery had been stripped of its contents. The other buildings of the Inner and Outer Courts may already have been demolished for their materials as surplus to requirements, even if the church were to become a cathedral, but only excavation will demonstrate this. Because Gresham had bought the site and its home estates for investment, he had no interest in building himself or his tenant a house out of the ruins, and Fountains was spared the destruction that resulted on so many other monastic sites. It is largely because he only carried out the work he was required to do that Fountains remains one of the most complete Cistercian monasteries of the medieval period.

The building of Fountains Hall

The abbey buildings and part of the home estates were sold by Gresham's son, Sir Thomas, to Stephen Proctor, son of Thomas Proctor, an early ironmaster, in 1597. Knighted in 1604 he acquired the lucrative post of Collector of Fines on Penal Statutes in 1606, and generally annoyed his neighbours by engaging them in endless lawsuits over land and mineral rights and by his relentless persecution of Catholics after the Gunpowder Plot of November 1605, the only zealous Protestant squire in a generally Catholic area. He built himself a small house, Fountains Hall, on the north side of the abbey precinct between the Outer and Inner gatehouses traditionally in or about 1611, but it must have been substantially complete by 1604 when the infant Prince Charles (later Charles I) and his retinue stayed there. The house (**80**) is a variant on Robert Smythson's design for Woolaton, and it is likely that Smythson provided designs, though he certainly did not oversee the building. Stylistic links can be made with other Smythson houses, notably Chastleton, Pontefract and Hardwick. It is a house of a single, tall facade, terraced into the valley side to increase its dramatic effect. Five storeys high and framed by square battlemented turrets, it is a strangely old-fashioned house hiding behind a fine renaissance front. The hall occupied the ground floor above a basement, with the Great Chamber above, its windows filled with armorial glass by Dinninghof reflecting Proctor's pretensions to gentility.

The house had cost Proctor some £3000 to build although he had been able to take stone from the abbey ruins. Perhaps it was his Protestant distaste for Rome that stopped him taking the best stone of the church and cloister buildings. Instead, he took stone from the abbot's house and infirmary and they owe their generally ruined state to his depredations. Infirmary stone, including a thirteenth-century string-course can be identified in the east wall of the house, and the arches over the entrance stairs are medieval and looted from somewhere in the abbey. More remarkably, the spiral stair from the south-west angle of the Nine Altars was removed almost totally, to be re-erected on the west side of the house. However, the greater part of the stone used appears to have been new-quarried, reducing the destruction of the medieval ruins that must have been an uncomfortable reminder of the country's Catholic past.

Sir Stephen Proctor died without an heir in 1619 and the abbey passed through a number of hands until it came into the possession of the Messenger family in the mid-seventeenth century. It was during their ownership that the historian Robert Thoresby visited the ruins in 1682 and described them as 'a noble wreck in ruinous perfection . . . full of trees in the very body of it'. Though they were Catholics, the Messengers appear to have done little to repair the ruins, but equally they did nothing to destroy them, and Fountains was reasonably safe in their hands until it was sold in 1767 to the owner of the adjoining estate of Studley Royal.

The clearance of the abbey ruins in the mid-nineteenth century brought to light some evidence of Civil War activity at Fountains. When the drain of the monks' latrine block was cleared out, a hoard of 354 silver pennies was found buried in the silt below the arch that carried the east wall of the abbot's chamber over the drain. These coins ranged in date from the reign of Mary Tudor up to the reign of Charles I, and had been placed where they might easily have been recovered. Presumably

80 *The south front of Fountains Hall with its wealth of Renaissance detailing hides what is essentially a rather old-fashioned house.*

whoever placed these coins there was unable to return and recover them. More graphic evidence was recovered when the walls that blocked off both ends of the sacristy on the south side of the south transept were removed to reveal 'a mass of human bones, sufficient according to a careful computation, to have formed not less than 400 skeletons'. At the time they were thought to have been bodies disturbed by the looting of medieval graves but recent excavation has shown that monastic burials that were disturbed were simply left lying about the site. More likely, such a cache represents the dead of a local Civil War action.

John Aislabie, the South Sea Bubble and the gardens of Studley Royal

To the east of Fountains in the Middle Ages was the village of Studley. By the third quarter of the seventeenth century it had long been deserted and was in the possession of George Aislabie, Registrar of the Ecclesiastical Court at York, as the inheritance of his wife Mary, the eldest daughter of Sir John Mallory. Their son, John Aislabie, inherited the Studley estate on his mother's death in 1699. Socially and politically ambitious, he was the Tory MP for Ripon, though he was to turn his coat and join the Whigs, becoming Chancellor of the Exchequer in 1718.

In 1711, the South Sea Company was formed to trade with the Spanish Americas, a trade which was mistakenly thought to be highly profitable. Speculation was rife, with many unscrupulous speculators obtaining subscriptions from the public to invest in the company. Shares rose dramatically in value and Aislabie was one of the sponsors of an Act of Parliament enabling people owed money by the state to convert their claims into South Sea shares. The share price rose from £100 to £1000 and then collapsed, causing widespread ruin. Disgraced, John Aislabie was expelled from Parliament and disqualified from holding public office for life. Wealthy but embittered, he returned to Yorkshire where he directed his considerable

81 *The remodelled valley of the river Skell seen from Aislabie's 'rustic bridge'.*

energies into the creation of a formal pleasure garden on his Studley Royal estate.

Work had actually begun on the garden in 1716 but the first phase, the creation of a new landscape, was not completed until 1730. The Skell valley was drastically remodelled with the river itself diverted into a canal at the centre of the valley with geometric ponds formed to either side (**81**). At the western boundary of the estate where the canal joined the unimproved Skell, a half-moon pond was created to act as a reservoir and Tent Hill, a conical mound, created to provide a vista. At the east end of the canal a new lake was created in Studley park, the junction marked by a cascade. The scale of the earthmoving was tremendous, with about 100 men employed seasonally under the direction of John Simpson. Additionally, seven contractors were employed to bring stone 6.4 km (4 miles) from Galphay Moor. The garden was designed by Aislabie himself, heavily infuenced by the great French formal gardeners such as le Nôtre, and by Queen Anne's gardeners George London and Henry Wise.

The garden buildings, all originally severely classical, were later additions to the design (**82**), and were built after 1732. Over ten years, two temples, an orangery (**83**), the Octagon Tower and various bridges were built. By Aislabie's death in 1742, the garden was largely complete. It formed a contrast to the abbey ruins that remained a vista at the west end of the gardens. Aislabie had originally intended to buy the Fountains estate from the Messengers, and a price of £4000 had been agreed when he suddenly withdrew. Perhaps he agreed with the traveller Arthur Young who concluded that 'ruins generally appear best at a distance'. In any case he had his vista (**84**). Indeed, the focus of Aislabie's most dramatic avenue along the drive from Studley to Ripon was the minster church there (**colour plate 12**), and it is instructive that so formal a landscape should have such imposing views of buildings that contrasted so strongly with the classical design of his own buildings.

82 *The Temple of Piety seen across Aislabie's canal, the circular Moon Pond and the Crescent Ponds.*

William Aislabie and Fountains Abbey

John Aislabie's son William inherited the Studley estate on his father's death in 1742, when the main work of the garden was complete. His contribution was to continue the landscaping of the lower Skell valley towards Ripon and to buy the Fountains estate in 1768 for the immense sum of £16,000. Tastes had changed since John Aislabie had designed his garden, and William broke away from formality to follow the picturesque approach which was to become the hallmark of Lancelot 'Capability' Brown in the last quarter of the eighteenth century. Fountains was no longer to be simply a vista, but the ruins were brought into the garden itself, set in an informal sweep of lawns and framed with trees (**85**).

83 *The Orangery, later refitted as a banqueting house was probably designed by Colen Campbell and built between 1728 and 1732.*

84 *Aislabie's vista of Fountains Abbey was painted by Balthazar Nebot in about 1760, before William Aislabie modified the landscape around the ruins (National Trust).*

The ruins were not quite to William Aislabie's taste, so they were improved, not simply by selective demolition but by the addition of new features. Gilpin, who visited in 1772 was not at all impressed by Aislabie's treatment of the ruins:

A few fragments scattered about the body of a ruin are proper and picturesque. They are proper because they account for what is defaced; and they are picturesque, because they unite the principal parts with the ground in which union the beauty of composition in a good measure depends. But here they are thought rough and unsightly, and fell a sacrifice to neatness . . . In the room of these detached parts, which are proper and picturesque embellishments of the scene, a gaudy temple is erected, and other trumpery wholly foreign to it. But not only the scene is defaced, and the *outworks of the ruin* violently torn away; *the main body of the ruin itself* is at this very time under the alarming hand of decoration. When the present proprietor made his purchase, he found the whole mass of ruins – the Cloisters, the Abbey Church, and the Hall – choked with rubbish. The first work therefore was to clear and open. And something in this way might have been done with propriety, for we see ruins sometimes so choked that no view of them can be obtained . . . But the restoration of parts is not enough: ornaments must be added [**86**], and such incongruous ornament, as disgrace the scene are disgracing also the monastery. The monks' garden is turned into a trim parterre and planted with flowering shrubs; a view is opened through the great window to some ridiculous I know not what (Anne Bolein I think they call it) that is planted in the valley; and in the central part of the abbey, a circular pedestal is raised out of fragments of the old pavement, on which is erected a mutilated heathen statue!'

85 *The ruins of Fountains Abbey in the informal landscape of the late eighteenth century.*

While Gilpin's complaints were largely a matter of taste, it is obvious that Aislabie did considerable damage to the archaeology and structure of the site. He swept away the remains of the elegant late twelfth-century cloister arcades, the tracery of the major windows of the church, and removed the arcades from the presbytery. There he reduced the ground level, destroying what remained of John of Kent's tile pavement and the open arcades that enclosed the altar space. He also spread fallen masonry about the site to establish levels for his all-pervading lawns, removing architectural detail from its original context and burying the bases of the piers in the nave and the shattered ruins of the abbot's house and infirmary. We are fortunate that antiquaries had already begun to show an interest in the ruins, and a plan was made for Burton's *Monasticon Eboracense* before Aislabie began his 'improvements' (**87**). There was of

86 *William Aislabie constructed a 'shrine' below the east window of the Chapel of the Nine Altars from a mixture of thirteenth-century and new arcading, recorded before it was removed by Walbran in the 1850s.*

course a positive side to Aislabie's acquisition of the ruins. As they were meant to adorn his landscape they had to be made secure. Repairs were frequently carried out to the fabric for the first time since 1539 which ensured the continuing survival of what remained, and the architectural elements of the parts he destroyed were spread about the site to be recovered in more recent times when they were more generally appreciated.

On Aislabie's death in 1781, his estate passed to his daughter Mrs Allanson who was persuaded by John Martin of Ripon to allow the excavation of the chapter-house. Martin had read Burton's *Monasticon* and believed that he would find the burials of important abbots there. The estate gardener was commissioned to dig the room out in 1790–1, and indeed the graves of the presidents from Richard of Clairvaux to William Rigton were revealed. In the course of this excavation, one of the earliest on any monastic site, the method of destruction of the chapter-house was revealed. The monolithic marble piers had been cut to take wedges that were driven in to crack the stone, ropes were then attached to the piers and horses or

oxen used to pull the columns out allowing the vault to fall. The excavation of 1790 recovered the greater part of the vault, which was simply carted out into the cloister where it remained until 1851, obscuring the chapter-house facade.

Fountains Abbey in the nineteenth century

In 1808, Mrs Allanson's niece, Mrs Lawrence, inherited the estate, and began a lengthy campaign of repair. In 1822 the southern part of the vault of the west range fell and was reconstructed. Excavation has revealed the evidence for shoring put up to support what had survived the fall. This shows that great care was taken to preserve what remained of the historic fabric and it is only the mortar used for the repair that identifies the new building.

In 1840, it was found that the transverse arches of the aisle vaults in the church were in

87 *The earliest plan of the ruins was made by T. Greaves for Dr John Burton's* Monasticon Eboracense *before William Aislabie modified the site.*

need of repair before they too fell. Scaffolding was required and holes were dug into the uneven surface left by Aislabie's dumping of material in the nave. Richard Walbran, an antiquarian and archaeologist from Ripon, was quick to see the potential revealed by these excavations:

> In clearing away, at that time, the mounds of rubbish that had accumulated in the southern aisle, the great square base of one of the columns of the nave was accidentally exposed; and on following it down to the floor, a singular and early geometrical painted pavement, apparently the floor of a chapel, was observed near the door leading to the Cloister Court. A few more openings were afterwards made, almost at random, in different parts of the church.

So began the serious archaeological study of the site. The workmen found a large grave-stone (see **52**), believed to be that of Abbot John Ripon at the time, between the eastern crossing piers, and lifted it to reveal 'the perfect skeleton of a very tall man . . . resting on a paved bed immediately below the stone; but no trace of a ring, chalice, paten, or any other relic or substance whatever was observed.' Mrs Lawrence, a Roman Catholic, was appalled by this sacrilege and Walbran's work was abruptly terminated.

Mrs Lawrence died in 1845, and in the following year the Royal Archaeological Institute, holding its summer meeting in Leeds visited the abbey with Walbran as the guide. He outlined his previous work and made the case for the continuing excavation of the site. The Earl de Grey, the new owner of the estate, was faced with continuing repair, this time to the tunnels that carried John of Kent's no longer visible infirmary over the Skell, and Walbran was invited to conduct prior excavation. This project began in November 1848 and was carried out with remarkable attention to detail.

Walbran mistook the building he was excavating for the abbot's house, an easy mistake to make at a time when the buildings of any monastery were not fully understood, and his error has coloured his interpretation but not invalidated his work. His observations were remarkably acute for the mid-nineteenth century and his approach was strangely modern: 'as the ground plan may be easily defined, and important fragments of the superstructure

were found within the area, a tolerably accurate idea of its former appearance can be obtained.' The masonry he recovered was carefully stacked to the south-west of the infirmary hall where it remained until 1988, and it can still be studied in the context of Walbran's published description of the excavation. It was Walbran who discovered that the infirmary hall had been subdivided in the late fifteenth and sixteenth centuries and that Tudor windows had been inserted to light the new apartments. His attention to detail is more apparent when he was dealing with non-structural evidence. Between the misericord and the infirmary passage (sec **58**) he found a yard where 'the last supply of coal that the house had needed remained under the sward' below which was a thick deposit of domestic rubbish, treasure trove to an archaeologist. Here

> . . . there was a silver spoon, weighing an ounce, with a capacious bowl, slender octagonal stem, and a head similar to an inverted Tudor bracket. Then broken pottery ware that had disappeared from the abbot's table, to the large coarse home-made jugs that after 'a mere crack' had been broken in the kitchen; a small silver ornament in the shape of a lion's face, apparently detached from a larger object; a silver ring; a broad brass ring; a copper can; a sickle blade; several Nuremberg tokens; part of a small ornament in lead, resembling the tracery of a Tudor window, and proving the application of architectural forms to domestic utensils; a quantity of beef, mutton, pork, and venison bones, together with those of poultry, herons, and other game; with bushels of oyster, mussel, and cockle shells, so fresh and pearly as when they left Abbot Bradley's table.

This was the waste from the misericord, testimony of the diet of the late Cistercian monks. Walbran found in these items the close connection he sought with people who were already so well known to him from a lifetime's study of the abbey's documents, and so it was that he recorded them so lovingly, to the extent that many objects can still be identified today. By the spring of 1850 the whole of the infirmary was exposed and some of its fallen masonry reset for display (**88**).

The 1850 season saw Walbran's attention turn to the ruins of the real abbot's house and

88 *Walbran reset two piers in the infirmary that he had found in a fallen state.*

the monks' latrines, buried to a depth of 2m (6ft) below a raised parterre and which were only partly known from Burton's plan (see **87**). In the process of excavating the prison cells below the abbot's hall he encountered the latrine drain of Murdac's monastery where 'the stench was so intolerable as to require quicklime to be thrown in before it could be cleaned out' destroying environmental evidence that had survived from the 1140s. Walbran had now revealed parts of the monastery lost to view since the seventeenth century and had established with de Grey a new approach to laying out the abbey ruins, no longer in the romantic fashion of the late eighteenth century but to suit the more precise taste of the mid-nineteenth century with its accurate approach to medieval architecture (**89**). The treatment was thus established for the rest of the site, changing the ruins from an object of curiosity to a stripped exposition of medieval architecture without the evidence of decay.

89 *The site following Walbran's excavation was stripped of fallen debris and had taken on much of its present-day appearance. In the foreground is the basement of the abbot's house, excavated by Walbran in 1850.*

Walbran turned his attention once more to the church in 1851, beginning at the south end of the Nine Altars and working westwards, an operation which required the installation of a light railway that ran out through the west door of the nave and was not completed until late in 1853. His objective was to clear the church to floor level and recover the evidence of floors, graves and missing structural parts. In this he was only partially successful, for Aislabie had removed the floor and arcades of the presbytery, and his workmen did not have the skills of present day archaeologists. In the Nine Altars he failed to find the grave of Abbot Gower but a burial was discovered above the floor level where Gower was known to be buried, the evidence of some post-suppression tragedy. It was not until he reached the crossing that he began to find what he was looking for. First to be revealed was the ledger of Abbot Swinton which he had first seen in 1840. Next came the transepts where floors survived and he discovered the grave slab of brother John Ripon and an unmarked slab in the south-west corner of the north transept, perhaps covering the burial of Abbot Huby robbed of its superstructure. In the south transept his workmen emptied a robbed grave before the northern chapel, exposing as they went masonry of the first stone church that Walbran failed to recognize. In the southern chapel he found quantities of masons' chippings, evidence of stone being reworked there after the suppression. The southern chapel had been cleared out in 1849 with only the discovery of a fragmentary tile pavement which had been laid by John of Kent. In the crossing, the accidental sinking of a wheelbarrow wheel revealed the presence of the acoustic pits beneath the choir stalls, but of the grave slabs of the abbots buried there, there was no trace. By the excavation of the nave 'little information was obtained' though up to 1.3m (4ft) of debris was removed to expose the bases of the piers. At the west end, however, 'two blocks of limestone, each two feet three inches square, with a circle inscribed on the surface, were found inserted in the floor, which led to a more particular examination, ending in the discovery of fifty of similar character'. These were processional markers of Huby's time. Next the galilee porch was cleared and part of its fallen arcade re-assembled, the remainder being dumped in the east guest-house. Among the fallen debris that buried the porch was Darnton's statue of the Virgin and Child which was reset in its niche above the west window, completing the clearance of the church.

Walbran also cleared the main cloister ranges, removing the worst of Aislabie's 'heathen' decorations. A crab-apple press was brought from the west range and set on an old foundation at the centre of the cloister garth, and architectural fragments were laid out on the tops of low walls for display. Sadly, Walbran did not live to write a full account of his work. While working on his definitive study of the abbey's documents he suffered a serious stroke in April 1868 and died 12 months later. It was left to another remarkable man to record the buildings that Walbran had uncovered and brought to the nation's attention.

Arthur Reeve was an architectural assistant of William Burges who was engaged on the design and building of St Mary's Church at Studley Royal for the Marquis and Marchioness of Ripon from 1870. To learn about the detail of medieval architecture, Burges told Reeve that he could do no better than to study the buildings of Fountains Abbey. This he did, sponsored by the Marquis, recording not only in plan but also in elevation (**90**) all the visible remains of the abbey. This *tour de force* was undertaken from 1873 to 1876 at the Marquis' expense and the exquisite ink and colour wash drawings were kept in the library of Fountains Hall where they remained until 1966. They are now owned by English Heritage. Reeve began his work on the west range, where by his own admission he did not record every stone as he found it. However, by the time he moved on to the guest-houses in 1873 he had rectified that failing and his drawings are from then a true record of what he saw at a scale of 1:96. The most important aspect of Reeve's work was that he drew those parts of the site that Walbran had revealed and which had remained exposed but had not yet suffered any serious deterioration. He may also have done some excavation himself to clear partially buried walls, for his plan of the woolhouse (**91**), which he identified as the bakehouse, shows walls that Walbran had not investigated but which only survived a few courses high and must have been buried. Reeve did not publish his work until 1892 when he wrote a lengthy text to accompany his drawings and produced a series of reconstruction drawings based on his

111

90 *Reeve's drawing of the north arcade of the nave, crossing and Huby's tower as it was in 1876.*

original record (**92**). By delaying the publication of his work he was able to collaborate with the most competent monastic archaeologist of the late nineteenth century, Sir William St John Hope.

Hope, the Assistant Secretary of the Society of Antiquaries of London, undertook two seasons of excavation and research at Fountains in September of 1887 and 1888 on behalf of the Yorkshire Archaeological Society. His work was basically to follow up points that Walbran had established nearly forty years before, and to interpret the buildings in the light of his unrivalled knowledge of monastic sites. Hope was responsible for the recovery of the plan of the east end of Richard of Clairvaux's church, for resolving the partitioning of the church (see **27** and **49**) and for the recovery of the pre-fire west, south and east cloister ranges. His excavation was restricted to strate

gically placed trenches no more than 0.6m (2ft) wide that did remarkably little damage to the site's archaeology. It was at Fountains that he first established the general layout of a typical Cistercian monastery, an interpretation that remains valid today. His publication of the site in 1900 set a new standard in the presentation of monastic buildings, comparing the remains of Fountains with the remains of 'nearly all the Cistercian monasteries in this country'. His debt to Reeve and Walbran was great but he was the first person truly to understand the ruins and appreciate their importance both nationally and internationally. He was also instrumental in having the ivy that grew all over the ruins, a pet hate of his wherever he

91 *(Above right) The 'bake-house' and malt-house as they were recorded in plan by Arthur Reeve. The captions have been reset. Compare this plan with **77**.*

92 *(Below right) Reeve's elevations of the east wall of the east range, and his reconstruction of the chapter-house in its late twelfth-century form.*

93 *Repair of the parapets of Huby's tower were carried out in the 1930s without the modern requirement of scaffolding.*

went, removed to conserve the fabric and expose more of it for study. What he did not appreciate was that ivy actually protected the walls and the paint that remained on them.

Fountains Abbey today

The recent history of Fountains is basically one of repair and presentation to an increasing number of visitors. The site had been regularly open to paying visitors since the mid-nineteenth century but it remained in a dangerous condition. By the late 1920s the ruins were in a very worrying state, and though privately owned, the Office of Works was sufficiently concerned to undertake a study of the site and make recommendations to the estate regarding the necessary repairs. The estate, grant-aided by the Office of Works, began a campaign of repairs that made the buildings safer and stopped further deterioration, employing a permanent team of stone masons (**93**). This continued until 1966 when the estate was sold to the West Riding County Council who placed the abbey ruins in the guardianship

of the Ministry of Public Buildings and Works. Ownership passed to North Yorkshire County Council after local government reorganization in 1973, and North Yorkshire in turn sold the Studley Royal estate to the National Trust in 1983. Today, the ruins are conserved by English Heritage, the lineal successor of the old Office of Works.

Being in the guardianship of the state, the abbey ruins have an assured future, and since 1966 a full programme of conservation and repair has been in progress. This work will not be fully completed until 2010. The conservation of ancient monuments, however, has a down side. Inevitably the evidence of historic fabric is altered as new stone is inserted to replace stone that has failed or been seriously eroded, and as old and decayed mortar pointing is renewed. Ground disturbance to repair failed foundations or to install power cables and land-drains, both necessary for the presentation of the site to an increasingly sophisticated public is destructive of buried archaeological deposits. Equally, buildings that were meant to have roofs remain at risk from the elements when the roofs are removed, with the loss of once crisp architectural detail and paint and plaster from exposed wall-surfaces. Consequently, any

94 *The excavation of the woolhouse in 1977–80 was the first major archaeological project to be undertaken at Fountains since the mid-nineteenth century and began the current intensive study of the site.*

conscientious attempt to maintain the ruins has to be coupled with a recording of the evidence that survives before it is modified or lost. At Fountains, this has meant having to have archaeologists and architectural historians recording the fabric before it is repaired and advising on the least destructive methods of conservation. Without that record, this book could not have been written.

Excavation began in 1968 in advance of a scheme to install floodlights to improve the presentation of the monument, a decision taken by the Minister of Works himself. Trenches were dug in all parts of the site, revealing for the first time that there were deep deposits below the levels exposed by Walbran and Hope. Hope's recording of the mid-twelfth-century east end of the church and of the first phase of the west range was confirmed, and

cables were routed so as not to damage buried walls. Unfortunately, the cable trenches did damage buried features, as later excavation was to prove. It is unlikely, however, that there would have been further excavation if the potential of the site had not been demonstrated by the digging of the cable trenches.

It was not until 1977 that large-scale excavation was undertaken, beginning with the site of Reeve and Hope's bake-house. There, low walls were exposed for the nineteenth-century excavation trenches had not been backfilled. They needed to be conserved but that could not be done until the site had been re-excavated (**94**). The result was to prove that considerable amounts of information could be recovered from a building which had been badly disturbed in the last century, and the building was at last correctly identified as the abbey's woolhouse (see **76** and **77**). From there, attention was turned to the south transept of the abbey church in 1979 when a problem of drainage was identified. Excavation there recovered the plan of two earlier churches, one of timber and one of stone. The stone church had been seen in two small trenches in 1968 but too little was visible

115

95 *Open University students recording a partially blocked window in the east wall of Abbot Murdac's dormitory range as part of the long-term recording of the abbey's historic fabric (Keith Emerick).*

to make anything of it. By 1980, the true significance of the buildings was apparent. There was not one monastery on the site but three, and a detailed study of the ruins and further excavation would reveal the story of the site's development. As a result, the south end of the early west range was excavated in 1987 when the river tunnels that carried the south end of its successor were repaired, and the northern part of the east range was examined in 1988–9. In 1987, the east guest-house was excavated in advance of its consolidation and display.

The detailed recording of upstanding masonry began with a survey of the mill in 1984 (see **74**), in greater detail than attempted by Reeve and with the intention of analysing its development. This was then extended, first to parts of the precinct wall that were to be repaired, the medieval river walls that canalized the Skell and the standing cloister buildings (**95**) and church. As well as recording the stonework, the drawings produced detailed evidence of mortars, painted decoration, masons' marks and the evidence of scaffolding. In time, they will provide the evidence for a full analysis of the ruins and their modification through time, taking the archaeological study of the site from below ground level to the very tops of the walls. Quite simply, Fountains will be the best known and understood medieval monastic site in the world.

Fountains will remain a site to enjoy, a feature in the landscape that is a monument not only to those who built it, but to the succeeding generations who despoiled it, modified it, cared for it and studied it. They have all left their marks indelibly in the structure of the ruins. Its future is assured, its ruins accessible to all.

Fountains Abbey and other sites to visit

The north of England is particularly rich in the ruins of Cistercian abbeys, of which Fountains is by far the best preserved though not necessarily the most informative. Taken together, these sites provide a clear picture of the rigorous reformed monasticism that the order introduced into England, its scale, its aestheticism, and its wealth. In addition to Fountains, seven other sites are open to the public. Other sites mentioned in the text lie on private land and can only be visited by prior arrangement.

Fountains Abbey
Fountains Abbey lies 6.4km (4 miles) to the south-west of Ripon in North Yorkshire, on the south side of the B6265 to Pately Bridge. The abbey ruins lie on the Studley Royal Estate which is owned by the National Trust, and can be visited every day of the year except Christmas Day. There is a charge for admission.

Visitors have access to the greater part of the abbey ruins which are still undergoing a programme of first-time consolidation and may be closed for reasons of safety. There is no public access to the mill which remains to be conserved or to most of the Outer Court and precinct wall, though both can be seen from the central area of the site. The only home grange to which there is public access is Swanley, the site of the National Trust's visitor centre. There is a small museum at the entrance to the Inner Court which contains an impressive (if slightly inaccurate) model of the main abbey buildings as they might have appeared in 1539, and some of the finer architectural material recovered from the site in nineteenth-century excavations.

The public can also visit the early seventeenth-century Fountains Hall, and the eighteenth-century park and gardens of Studley Royal, within which lies the nineteenth-century church of St Mary, Studley Royal, managed by the National Trust on behalf of English Heritage and open only in the summer months.

Rievaulx Abbey
Fountains' great rival, Rievaulx Abbey, lies 5km (3 miles) to the west of Helmsley in North Yorkshire to the south of the B1257 to Stokesley, 48 km (30 miles) from Fountains. Substantial ruins of the church and cloister buildings remain and are in the care of English Heritage. The site is open every day of the year except Christmas Day, and there is a charge for admission. In the visitor centre there is a small exhibition that concentrates on the Cistercian mission to Yorkshire and the early history of the abbey.

Rievaulx is a more complex site than Fountains and is more heavily ruined. Its buildings, however, are much more informative for more detail has survived. This is particularly true of the church and dormitory range. In addition to the church and claustral ranges, the village church, still in use, incorporates the remains of the gate chapel and parts of the inner gatehouse remain in the churchyard boundary. The buildings of the Inner and Outer Courts lie under the post-suppression village that clusters to the west of the church and one mill, substantially rebuilt, survives, though it is now a private house. The remainder of the precinct is farmland to which limited access can be gained by public footpaths.

Furness Abbey
The third great Cistercian monastery in the north was Furness Abbey, the ruins of which survive 3km (2 miles) north of Barrow in Fur-

ness in Cumbria, on the east side of the A590. The site is managed by English Heritage and is open all year apart from Christmas Day. There is an entry charge.

The principal surviving buildings are the church, east range, abbot's house, and infirmary, though the whole precinct survives within parkland surrounded by a well-preserved precinct wall with two surviving gatehouses. Additionally, the gate chapel and the low walls of the inner gatehouse survive, and a roofed building, apparently part of a water-mill, remains in the southern part of the precinct. This is not open to the public. The visitor centre contains an exhibition on the history and economy of the abbey and a display of tomb-covers and architectural detail.

Kirkstall

Fountains' daughter house of Kirkstall lies in public parkland to the north-west of Leeds adjacent to the A65 and close to Headingley station. The site is managed by Leeds City Council which maintains a museum in the intact inner gatehouse.

The church and cloister ranges are well preserved, and for the most part are contemporary with Abbot Richard of Clairvaux's buildings at Fountains. To the west of the cloister are the substantial remains of the guest-hall, and much of the precinct, now bisected by the A65, can be identified from its earthworks.

Roche Abbey

A grand-daughter of Fountains, Roche Abbey lies on the south side of the A634 between Maltby and Blyth in South Yorkshire. The site is managed by English Heritage, and is open to the public between Easter and the end of September. There is a charge for admission.

At the entrance to the site are the substantial remains of the inner gatehouse, though all the buildings of the inner and outer courts have disappeared below parterres laid by Capability Brown in the late eighteenth century. Brown similarly levelled and buried the greater part of the church and cloister ranges, though these have been excavated and displayed. The principal survival is the east wall of the transepts, which survive to full height as they were used as a landscape feature, the quality of which shows why the abbey buildings were described as 'magnificent' in the fourteenth century.

Sawley Abbey

A grand-daughter of Fountains, Sawley or Salley Abbey lies on the north side of the A59 to the north-east of Clitheroe in Lancashire. Its ruins are managed by English Heritage and are open without charge at any reasonable time.

The transepts and first bay of the nave survive to reasonable height, together with the lower walls of an extended presbytery, and the cloister ranges remain largely as low walling. To the north, east and south of the site, on private land, are substantial earthworks which define the precinct. These can largely be seen from the ruins.

Byland Abbey

Founded from Furness via Calder Abbey, Byland Abbey moved to its third and final site in 1177. The site lies to the south of the A170 between Helmsley and Thirsk, close to the village of Coxwold in North Yorkshire. The ruins are managed by English Heritage, and are open to the public every day of the year except for Christmas Day. There is a charge for admission.

Substantial remains of the church and cloister ranges are set within a large precinct (largely on private land) defined by good earthworks, many of which can be seen from the monument. Byland was architecturally distinguished, and a small museum on site displays some of the more important detail recovered by excavation in the 1920s.

Jervaulx Abbey

A daughter-house of Byland, Jervaulx Abbey lies on the east side of the A6108 between Masham and Middleham in North Yorkshire. The site is privately owned but the ruins are open to the public at any reasonable time. There is a charge for admission.

The ruins of Jervaulx, excavated in the first years of the nineteenth century and incorporated in a garden, are a delight. Unlike the other sites they have not been tidied up for display and architectural detail is stacked up close to where it was originally found. The church is heavily ruined, but much detail remains in the cloister ranges, the infirmary and the meat kitchen.

The abbots of Fountains

The story of Fountains Abbey is inevitably centred on the work and reputation of its abbots. A full list is known and is given below. The numbers they are given are the numbers they were accorded in the Middle Ages, and those who were not numbered were felt by the convent to have ruled unwisely or brought the monastery into disrepute. After their names a brief résumé of their previous careers, if known, is given, followed by the dates of their abbacies:

1	*Richard I*, prior of York	1132–1139
2	*Richard II*, sacrist of York, prior of Fountains	1139–1143
3	*Henry Murdac*, abbot of Vauclair, became archbishop of York 1147, died 1153	1144–1147
	Maurice, subprior of Durham, abbot of Rievaulx, resigned	1147–1148
	Thorold, monk of Rievaulx, resigned, became abbot of Trois Fontaines	1148–1150
4	*Richard III*, precentor of Clairvaux, abbot of Vauclair	1150–1170
5	*Robert of Pipewell*, abbot of Pipewell	1170–1180
6	*William of Newminster*, canon of Guisborough, abbot of Newminster	1180–1190
7	*Ralph Haget*, abbot of Kirkstall	1190–1203
8	*John of York*, cellarer of Fountains, abbot of Louth Park	1203–1211
9	*John of Hessle*, became bishop of Ely	1211–1220
10	*John of Kent*, cellarer of Fountains	1220–1247
11	*Stephen of Eston*, cellarer of Fountains, abbot of Sawley, abbot of Newminster	1247–1252
12	*William of Allerton*, prior of Fountains	1253–1258
13	*Adam*	1258–1259
14	*Alexander*	1259–1265
15	*Reginald*	1265–1274
	Peter Ayling, resigned 1279, died 1282	1274–1279
16	*Nicholas*	1279
17	*Adam Ravensworth*	1280–1284
	Henry Otley, probably resigned 1289, died 1290	1284–1289
	Robert Thornton, probably resigned 1290, died 1306	1289–1290
18	*Robert Bishopton*	1290–1311
19	*William Rigton*	1311–1316
20	*Walter Coxwold*, resigned 1336, died 1338	1316–1336
21	*Robert Copgrove*	1336–1346
22	*Robert Monkton*	1346–1369
23	*William Gower*, resigned 1384, died 1390	1369–1384
24	*Robert Burley*	1384–1410
	Roger Frank, monk of Fountains, deposed 1413	1410–1413
25	*John Ripon*, cellarer of Fountains, abbot of Meaux	1414–1435
26	*Thomas Paslew*, resigned 1442, died 1443	1435–1442
27	*John Martin*	1442
28	*John Greenwell*, monk of Fountains, abbot of Waverley, commissary of the abbot of Cîteaux	1442–1471
29	*Thomas Swinton*, prior of Fountains, resigned 1478	1471–1478

30 *John Darnton*, cellarer of Fountains, commissary of the abbot of Cîteaux 1479–1495

31 *Marmaduke Huby*, monk, bursar, and cellarer of Fountains, master of St Mary Magdalene hospital, and commissary of the abbot of Cîteaux 1495–1526

32 *William Thirsk*, commissary of the abbot of Cîteaux, resigned 1536, executed 1537 1526–1536

33 *Marmaduke Bradley*, monk of Fountains, prebendary of Thorpe, master of St Mary Magdalene hospital, surrendered his abbey to the Crown in 1539, died 1553 1536–1539

Further reading

Because of its exceptional nature, Fountains Abbey is one of the most studied and published monastic sites in Europe and the reader is somewhat spoiled for choice. However, as the site is still being researched it is always wise to treat older publications with a degree of caution.

For background reading, the best introduction to the Cistercians in the north of England is P.J. Fergusson, *The Architecture of Solitude* (Princeton 1984). For the earliest buildings of the order in England see R. Halsey 'The earliest architecture of the Cistercians in England' in C. Norton and D. Park (eds.) *Cistercian Art and Architecture in the British Isles* (Cambridge 1986). This volume also contains a second paper by C. Wilson, 'The Cistercians as "missionaries of Gothic" in northern England' which places the thirteenth-century development of Fountains in its wider context. A general description of the site itself can be found in four places: G.M. Hill, 'Fountains Abbey, Yorkshire' in *Collectanea Archaeologica* 2 (1871); W. St John Hope's 'Fountains Abbey' in the *Yorkshire Archaeological Journal* 15 (1900); in A.W. Oxford *The Ruins of Fountains Abbey* (London 1910); and R. Gilyard-Beer *Fountains Abbey* (London 1984). These four works record the developing interpretation of the site and demonstrate the largely historical and architectural approach to the ruins.

Particular aspects of the site have been examined in more detail. The timber phase of the monastery has been placed in context in P. Fergusson: 'The first architecture of the Cistercians in England and the work of Abbot Adam of Meaux', *Journal of the British Archaeological Association* 136, (1983), and the first stone monastery buildings initially discussed by R. Gilyard-Beer in 'Fountains Abbey, the early buildings, 1132–50' in *Archaeological Journal* 125 (1968). This paper has been substantially revised by more recent research described in R. Gilyard-Beer and G. Coppack 'Excavations at Fountains Abbey, North Yorkshire, 1979–80: the early development of the monastery' in *Archaeologia* 108 (1986). The excavation of the woolhouse in the Outer Court is described in G. Coppack: 'The excavation of an Outer Court building, perhaps the Woolhouse, at Fountains Abbey, North Yorkshire' in *Medieval Archaeology* 30, 1986. For Richard Walbran's excavations of the mid-nineteenth century, there are summary reports in J. Raine (ed.) 'Memorials of Fountains Abbey II', *Surtees Society* 67, 1876. Further accounts of his work can be found in J.R. Walbran's *Guide to Ripon* 1862 and earlier editions. An English text of the *Narratio de fundatione Fontanis monasterii* can be found in Oxford's *The Ruins of Fountains Abbey*, and in its Latin text in J.R. Walbran (ed.) 'Memorials of Fountains Abbey I', *Surtees Society* 42, 1842.

For the abbey estates, the basic material is to be found in W.T. Lancaster (ed.) 'Abstracts of the Charters and Other Documents Contained in the Chartulary of the Cistercian Abbey of Fountains', 2 vols (Leeds 1915). For granges generally and Cowton in particular, see C. Platt *The Monastic Grange in Medieval England* (London 1969). For a recent review of the monastic economy in northern England see S. Moorhouse: 'Monastic estates, their composition and development' in R. Gilchrist and H. Mytum (eds.) 'The Archaeology of Rural Monasteries', *British Archaeological Reports British Series*, 203 (1989).

Glossary

antiphonary A church service book which contains verses of the psalms and other traditional passages from the scriptures which were sung as responses (antiphons), often alternating between groups of choir monks.

apse The rounded termination of a chapel, aisle or east end of a church or similar building, normally of eleventh- and twelfth-century date.

arcade A series of arches carried on columns, as for instance between the main vessel of a church and an aisle, that carries the superstructure of the building.

ashlar Square-cut stone laid in regular courses to make the face of a wall.

bay The structural division of a building, normally emphasized in its architecture by vertical divisions, the placing of columns and buttresses.

bercary From the Latin *bercaria* a monastic sheep ranch, signifiying not simply buildings but pastures and enclosures in open country.

buttress The localized widening of a wall at its bay divisions to provide additional support against the outward pressure exerted by roofs and vaults in a masonry building.

bloomery A furnace for the smelting of iron ore.

capital The decorative top to a column which carries the springing of the arches of an arcade, often highly carved and painted, or similarly the decorated top of a wall or nook-shaft.

carucate A unit of land that could be tilled by one plough in a season generally between 48.5 and 56.5 ha (120 and 140 acres).

clerestory The upper storey of an aisled building, particularly a church, which was provided with windows to light the central vessel.

corbel A stone bracket, often carved, that projected from a wall-face to support either timber-work, a wall-shaft or the ribs of a vault.

crossing The point at which the principal axes of a cruciform church met at the junction of nave, presbytery and transepts. Normally it was architecturally marked by a tower, and it was the preferred location of the monks' choir-stalls.

garth An enclosed yard or paddock, normally associated with particular buildings, for instance the bakehouse garth or stable garth.

interdict The prohibition by a Pope or bishop of a person, institution, diocese or country of the celebration of divine service within churches and chapels.

jamb The side of a door or window frame.

laver A washing place, normally placed in the cloister but sometimes also in the infirmary and other buildings, supplied with a piped water-supply, and often distinguished by its architectural sophistication.

lay brother A monastic servant subject to the same discipline as the choir-monks but unlettered and responsible for the day-to-day servicing of the community. They comprised the major element in early Cistercian monasteries where they were used to farm substantial estates, but most orders actually had them in small numbers.

mark A currency of account rather than of coin which was valued at 13s 4d (£0.66)

nave The central vessel of an aisled building. In the monastic church it signifies the long or western arm of the church which might be partly used by the laity or by lay brothers.

parclose A wooden screen, often with elaborate decoration, that was used to divide a chapel from the main body of the church, or to divide chapels from each other.

pentice A passage or corridor running along the side of a building, its single-pitch (or pent) roof being carried on corbels in the wall of that building. Such corridors were normally of light construction and have left little trace.

pier A free-standing masonry column that supports an arcade.

presbytery The eastern arm of a monastic church that contained the enclosure of the high altar to the east of the monks' choir-stalls.

pulpitum The screen that closed the west end of the monks' choir-stalls, either of stone or timber.

quarry A cut piece of window glass of regular shape, often in the form of a square or diamond, that was fitted into a leaded framework to make up a decorative pattern. The word comes from the norman French 'carré' which means 'squared'.

respond A half-pier placed against a wall at the end of an arcade.

retable A shelf or frame enclosing decorated panels above the back of an altar.

rood screen The screen that closes off the nave from the monks' part of the church, normally set directly to the east of the nave altar, with doors through it to either side of the altar. There was normally a loft over it which carried images of the Holy Virgin, St John and Christ crucified, which themselves constituted the 'rood'.

simony The buying or selling of any church office, and by extension, the buying or selling of church property.

string-course A horizontal moulding used to level up the coursing of rubble walls and to mark the structural divisions of elevations, for instance at window cill level or below a parapet.

transept The north and south arms of a cruciform church to either side of the crossing, and called the 'cross aisle' in medieval sources. They provided additional space for chapels.

transom The horizontal division of lights in a multi-light window.

undercroft A vaulted ground-floor or semi-subterranean room, of secondary importance to the room above and often used only for storage.

vaccary From the Latin *vaccaria*, a monastic cattle ranch, its buildings, paddocks, and pastures.

vault The fire-proof ceiling of a room. Vaults vary greatly in complexity, from simple barrel vaults to elaborate ceilings divided into panels by decorative and moulded ribs.

wayleave An agreement with a neighbouring landowner or his tenant to move stock and produce across land that was under his control or management. Such arrangements were common in the Middle Ages when the present network of public roads did not exist and land was often difficult of access.

Index

(Page numbers in **bold** refer to illustrations)